The Life of a School

Studies in the Postmodern Theory of Education

Shirley R. Steinberg
General Editor

Vol. 423

The Counterpoints series is part of the Peter Lang Education list.
Every volume is peer reviewed and meets
the highest quality standards for content and production.

PETER LANG
New York • Washington, D.C./Baltimore • Bern
Frankfurt • Berlin • Brussels • Vienna • Oxford

Ivor F. Goodson & Christopher J. Anstead

The Life of a School

A Research Guide

PETER LANG
New York • Washington, D.C./Baltimore • Bern
Frankfurt • Berlin • Brussels • Vienna • Oxford

Library of Congress Cataloging-in-Publication Data
Goodson, Ivor F.
The life of a school: A research guide / Ivor F. Goodson, Christopher J. Anstead
p. cm. — (Counterpoints: studies in the postmodern theory of education; vol. 423)
Includes bibliographical references and index.
ISBN 978-1-4331-1435-9 (hardcover)
ISBN 978-1-4331-1434-2 (paperback)
ISBN 978-1-4539-0246-2 (e-book)
ISSN 1058-1634

Bibliographic information published by **Die Deutsche Nationalbibliothek**
Die Deutsche Nationalbibliothek lists this publication in the "Deutsche
Nationalbibliografie"; detailed bibliographic data is available
on the Internet at http://dnb.d-nb.de/.

The paper in this book meets the guidelines for permanence and durability
of the Committee on Production Guidelines for Book Longevity
of the Council of Library Resources.

© 2012 Peter Lang Publishing, Inc., New York
29 Broadway, 18th floor, New York, NY 10006
www.peterlang.com

All rights reserved.
Reprint or reproduction, even partially, in all forms such as microfilm,
xerography, microfiche, microcard, and offset strictly prohibited.

Printed in the United States of America

CONTENTS

Chapter 1	Introduction: Studying the Life of a School	1
	SECTION 1	
Chapter 2	Discovering Qualitative Sources	9
Chapter 3	Investigating Quantitative Sources	22
Chapter 4	Collecting Oral Sources	27
	SECTION 2	
Chapter 5	Developing a Narrative Overview	39
Chapter 6	Inside a Research Project: Episodes from a Methodological Diary	51
Chapter 7	Conjunctures and Critical Incidents	87
Chapter 8	Curriculum History	97
Chapter 9	Studying School Subjects: Patterns of Gender and Class	112
Chapter 10	Studying the Everyday Life of a School	127

Notes   145

References   147

CHAPTER ONE

Introduction

Studying the Life of a School

In the past decade or so, there has been an increasing interest in employing a combination of archival and life history methods to understand the complexities of schooling. This book uses our own exploration of the history of a particular school (Beal Technical School) to discuss the methods and problems of researching the story of a school. It seeks to offer the new researcher a series of practical guidelines and examples for doing such research. At the same time, it includes elements of the case history of a case study, leading to an extended discussion of complex issues of representation which will hopefully be of interest to the new and the more experienced educational researcher.

The introduction is quite short, with just a brief description of the project, but after describing the format of the book, it explains why we chose to write it.

Each of the chapters in section 1 includes an introduction to the range of possible resources, a reflective description of our own experiences, and some suggestions to others. Discussion includes thoughts on the biased nature of all sources and questions on the nature of source survival. Besides discussion, it will be important to include examples of original sources.

Each of the chapters in section 2 comprises at least one representation that we have constructed from the history of Beal and discussions of the process by which it was constructed. We are thereby trying to provide examples of different ways of representing the school and in doing so, we illustrate how the particular nature and form of our sources affect our subsequent accounts.

Chapter 5 tells a conventional historical narrative which covers the broad sweep of the school's history. It is based primarily on traditional archival sources and also includes some statistical sections.

Chapter 6 discusses an approach based on critical incidents and provides an example based on one such incident in Beal's history. Discussion includes a search for sociological models and a review of the potential of methods of the Annaliste historians.

In chapter 6, we also talk through the details of "life inside a research project." There are few studies of the strange and compelling process conducted within research projects. Partly with this in mind, we decided that keeping a "methodological diary" would aid our reflexivity and offer insights into the research process for a wider audience.

In chapter 7, we go through the classroom door and examine a particular curricular subject as it was taught at Beal. Discussion of this reconstruction refers to recent developments in curriculum history and especially, to the social construction of the school subject (Goodson, 2009).

In chapter 8, we discuss the way in which popular memory constructs an alternative history of a school. Using a specific myth from Beal, we examine the collectivising ability of an institution and the repercussions this has on individual memory. We also touch on the role of newspapers in this regard.

Chapter 9 turns to a more vernacular reconstruction of the history of the school, one that emphasises the structuration of everyday experience. Discussion centres on the importance of including these sorts of reconstruction in historical studies and relating them to the understanding of oral history.

The conclusion talks about how the various representations of the history of a school are related and how it is vitally important to focus on the "everyday world" of schooling.

Methodological Entry Points

Single Events as a Narrative Style

The analysis of one event in the history of a school is a popular choice for historians of education (McCulloch, 2011; McCulloch & Richardson, 2000). A tale set in a limited scope of time, with a small group of actors, can be treated in an easily comprehensible text. A longer history, told through events, provides an eminently readable story. People tend to partly experience their own lives as a series of events, each with a particular place in time. As a narrative device, events tie into this human experience; events can be presented as a compact set of causes and outcomes with a beginning, middle, and end. As stories, they are complete in themselves, though they may have much longer-term causes or implications.

This sort of approach can highlight an event in a way that brings a much longer scope of history into foreshortened view, with the event being used as a springboard for extended discussion. Choosing events is the key decision to make in this type of approach. The choice may be driven by your theory: Definitions can give certain events theoretical purchase, or the choice may arise from reading the data—with the sources seeming to indicate that an event was important. In general, a combination of historical and ethnographic work tends to focus closely on reading the data (Comaroff & Comaroff, 1992).

The benefits of this kind of approach derive chiefly from the ability to focus your work. A specific incident provides a tremendous focal point for any general theoretical explanation. It is possible to go into a single action in exhaustive detail. To probe your interpretation, you can turn the incident on its head, analyse it in every way possible, and consult as many alternate readings as are available before placing yourself as an arbiter of the various claims on the past. You may even wish to explore the counterfactual—the "what-ifs."

The choice of a single event also provides focus for your research task. By choosing a particular time, place, and cast of characters, you limit the range of documents and other sources you have to survey to understand the issues at hand. Lengthy research processes, such as selecting informants or searching newspaper articles, could be shortened. At the same time, you can proceed much more deeply into the relevant sources. You can hunt down and unearth details that would be easily skipped in a broader approach to school history. You could easily find yourself with knowledge from all sides of an issue.

The most obvious drawback in this approach is the question of whether you have developed a meaningful story line and viable contextual location. If you only examine one event, how do you know how important it stands in relation to other events which occurred in the history of a given school? Beyond that, the setting of a specific, single context may limit the importance of your argument. It is crucial to include an examination of context in your description, but it is difficult in a single-event study to determine the degree to which events are contingent upon that context.

A study of short-term events is open to the criticism that it misses the long view. Readers may rightly question whether the fact that, for instance, a particular principal sponsored a particular curriculum initiative has substantial meaning in the overall history of that school. Historians who study broad economic and social structures often feel events are of minor importance, representing the acting out of preexisting imperatives.

As a final warning, if you do choose to focus all your energy on a single event, missing sources can present huge or insurmountable problems. If one actor remains an enigma (because she left no diary and no one else understood her), if the minutes of a controversial meeting are lost, or if a proposed curriculum scheme was tossed out once it was turned down, the basis of your whole interpretation may be jeopardised.

Representational Events

While a study of events can be justified by claiming that the events are important, it is also possible to base the claim on their capacity to be representative. A representative event is one which provides, in contained form, an illustration of long-term or widespread change. The event in itself may not be critical but provides understanding of critical change. Of course, to make this claim, you need to identify those broader patterns and make a convincing case for them. The degree of fit between your chosen incident and wider patterns is always at issue; readers may object that your chosen institution is not representative but simply the result of idiosyncratic actors and structures.

Critical Events

The alternative to justification based on representativeness is one based on the importance of a given event in itself. The starting point for discovering critical events is to simply search the sources for any reference to occurrences deemed important. Many—but not all—events which alter school history are outlined in press clippings, discussed in the official records of school boards, or commented upon in school newspapers or yearbooks. While it will be your job to judge whether contemporaries were right in attributing importance to a given action, the sources provide a very good starting point.

An alternate approach to identifying critical events involves looking for disjunctures in the discourse surrounding a school. On reading collections of school memoranda, yearbooks, or clippings, you may frequently find a lack of continuity between the rhetoric at one time and at a later time. Tracing back to the point where change first appears provides a milestone for finding critical events connected to the disjuncture.

The lived experience of people who had a day-to-day connection to the school provides an important measuring device for defining critical events. Experiential analysis of the life stories and oral histories collected by your research team is crucial. This sort of analysis can be carried on across lives—comparing those connected with the school before and after a suspected significant turning point. A comparison within the life story of someone who was linked to the school, both before and after, might be identified by you in collaboration with the subject (see Kincheloe, 2004, 2005; Kincheloe & Berry, 2004; Kincheloe & Steinberg,1997, 2007).

Once you have found your critical event, you must give some thought to justifying your choice. Probably the most obvious way to justify the choice of a particular event is to be able to point to significant long-term results. An event which changed the history of a school in a meaningful way should be obvious to all. If this is not true at a surface level, it is up to you to make it readily apparent to your readers. History provides us with hindsight—this is not just a truism, it is a powerful tool. Use it to judge the importance of events. Experiential analysis can also provide justification for your claims. If oral accounts suggest that the experiential nature of your school changed significantly at the time of your chosen event, this is compelling evidence.

Writing Critical Events Narratives

A crucial element in the telling of critical events narratives is the time spent setting the stage. For the meaning of a change to be understood, what went before must be shown. The constraints on actors, the structures of institutional life, the role of tradition—all of these pre-existing elements provide fodder for interpretation (Kincheloe, 2004, 2005; Kincheloe & Berry, 2004; Kincheloe & Steinberg, 2007).

Once you move into an examination of the particular incident, you must make sure you tell all sides of the story. A narrative of an event from the point of view of a single source is nothing more than chronicling. Instead, your job is to find the common ground and points of convergence among sources. You must attempt to oversee the conflicting tales and construct what you can from them. Your construction will probably not be able to take account of all interpretations, and you must mention those sources which provide versions incommensurable with your own narrative.

Event-based history tends to emphasise the role of heroes. Men (too often in the past, mystical "gentlemen") and women who acted in the context of their times to produce change, or react to it, provide the narrative impetus behind events. To be effective, the actors have to be present as rounded people, not mere caricatures of interested groups. In crafting an events-based history, then, you must be aware of the subtle nuances of personal history. People are not all self-aware, logically acting, unconstrained individuals. Instead, they are only partially aware of both their own motives and subconscious knowledges and the surrounding structures. They may act in ways which seem to contradict a rational assessment of their own interests. They constantly operate under an intricate network of constraints that stretch from their own sense of self, through social norms, to the regulatory apparatus of the state (Goodson & Lindblad, 2010).

Finding Conjunctures

In chapter 7, we define and employ the notion of conjunctures to develop an intersectional view of school (see Goodson, 2004, 2010).

There are two routes to identifying a conjuncture. First, you can approach the question by looking for an important event in the way described above and then seeing if it did in fact mark a conjuncture. A conjuncture provides actors with structures of opportunity. Once an important event has been suggested, analyse the trends at the other levels of time to see if the event did represent the seizing of opportunity. Of course, opportunity missed cannot be identified this way.

A second way is to work in the opposite direction, by identifying those periods when a conjuncture was possible. In this case, you have to decide what phenomena you see fitting into which type of time. Mind sets, trading cycles, and geography have traditionally been put into the category of long time and, thus, are unlikely to change in any study of recent educational history. Conjuncture occurs when several medium-term cycles enter coincidental periods of change. Thus, a way to search for conjuncture is to chart the medium-term cycles. Decide upon those cycles which are likely to have an effect on your chosen area of interest. These will be external to your school, operating at the level of local, regional, national, and international trends in things such as curriculum reform, educational structures, or resource allocations, as well as broader social and economic areas (Goodson & Hargreaves, 2006). Reconceptualising our study of curriculum change and school change along these lines offers a promising perspective for studying the life of a school.

From this historical base, we can move into the analysis of curriculum history and the painstaking reconstruction of the everyday life of the school. In this way, to paraphrase E. P. Thompson (1968), we can save the teachers and the students of school from the enduring "condescension of history."

SECTION ONE

CHAPTER TWO

Discovering Qualitative Sources

In this chapter, we hope to sketch out the range of possible qualitative resources, provide a reflective description of our own experiences, and make some suggestions to aid your own approach. In particular, we want to emphasize the inevitably biased and partial nature of all sources and the differential survival of historical sources.

Qualitative methods have become progressively influential in social research, and this is reflected in a burgeoning literature. A range of new journals reflect this trend—a wonderful source of methodological commentary in educational research is found in these, particularly the *International Journal of Qualitative Studies in Education*. More generally, the journal *Qualitative Inquiry* is invaluable. Perhaps the best guide to qualitative methods is that by Norman Denzin and Yvonna Lincoln (1998), but also of note is the standard guide by Miles and Huberman (1994).

Searching for Sources

Any researcher undertaking a historical study—including the study of a school—commences by determining the extent of primary material available for study. Official records may be kept by the institution in question, in the holdings of local boards of education, or at county, provincial/state, or national archives. Unofficial records can be sought in local libraries, archives, or museums. We are certainly aware that we are reporting on a school with a much richer, and indeed longer, archive than many schools. Nonetheless, scholars of schooling are often surprised by just how much material they can "dig out."

Beal Tech has maintained (more through inertia and ample storage space than any conscious plan) an interesting collection of documents relating to its early history. In addition, several years ago, a group of teachers at the school decided to celebrate the institution's seventy-fifth anniversary by exploring some of its history. As a result, they established a depository of mementos, now in virtually forgotten storage. This collection—stored rather haphazardly and without any thought to proper preservation techniques—includes several hundred photographs, a classroom notebook, and a scrapbook started by H.B.

Beal. The images in the photos and the notes in the notebook allowed us our first glimpse into the actual world of the classroom.

Beal's "archives" are not an official collection but instead, the ad hoc result of available space and the seventy-fifth anniversary movement. In our time of association at the school, they have been moved three times; they are not stored in a stable manner, nor are they easily retrievable. More than that, several people have expressed the hope that the archives will not simply be thrown out one day, while acknowledging that it is likely.

Records in public archives and libraries are generally open to public use, but to study records held at the school or board office, you have to consult authorities—head teachers or school board officials—and go back to them if your search changes direction. For instance, simply in looking around as he worked on student records in the Beal vault, Anstead saw a variety of boxes, volumes, and other records which seemed to cover broad periods of the school's history. We felt the need to seek permission to go into these sources, hoping that this would not be a controversial question since we already had access to student records. Still, you do not want to be in the position of rooting through locked-up documents without someone's specific permission to do so.

Beyond these more or less readily available documents, your research team may want to actively solicit the loan of written sources from former students and teachers at the school (possibly at the time you collect oral testimony). Absent from official sources is any information about what went on in the classroom. There are few notes on pedagogical practice or subject content, except in the broadest terms. Sources such as diaries, letters, and school yearbooks and magazines written by students; notes and other material written by teachers; and student notebooks, which do not normally show up in school archives, allow a much greater understanding of the school experience. This area will be the most fun to explore, but it is also crucial to understanding how things decided at other levels affect the classroom experience of students and teachers.

Though most sources will be available within your local area, province, or state, specific research questions may lead to long-distance research contacts. A letter (or e-mail message) is more efficient than a phone call in determining the location of particular pieces of information:

To Special Collections, Milbank Memorial Library Teachers College, Columbia University

```
Dear Sir or Madam,
I am writing in an attempt to obtain some information about
your collection, and to seek your aid in solving some
```

problems. I am currently engaged in a research project focussing on vocational education. In particular, we are studying curriculum change at a local vocational high school in the period from 1900 to 1940. In trying to understand the changes which this school experienced, we have come to the conclusion that we have to understand the beliefs of a single person. That person was Herbert Benson Beal, of London, Ontario, the school's founder and principal for two decades. Beal himself seems to have been greatly influenced by a course which he took at Teachers College. We would like to know more about this, but face some challenges. We do not know what course Beal took, or when he took it. We know that he attended the College (as a non-degree student) sometime between 1898 and 1912, possibly in 1908 or 1909.

Can your collection answer any of these questions for us? Do you have student records which would indicate when Beal attended, or what course he took? If we can determine the course, do you have outlines or student notebooks which we can examine? Finally, do you know of anyone currently studying the nature of the College at this time? We are aware of the book by L. Cremin et al., and of the work by Kliebard.

Thank-you very much for your help.

In this case, the response from Columbia University was both heartening and depressing. The staff at the archives there are quite willing to help. However, they could do nothing until we determined which course Beal took. To do this involved opening his academic records. An official in the registrar's office told us that only Beal's estate or heirs could make this request.

A central question always arises: Which sources are best? The earlier the period under study, the more your choices will be limited; for recent periods, you have to make decisions based at least partly on efficiency. A study of newspapers is interesting but might not be efficient enough. Other written (mainly official) sources would provide an overall picture more quickly but would reflect the values of either the teachers or external agencies. Still, the contrast between just those two groups can provide a fertile field for exploration and set much of the context for any study of individual classrooms. For this reason, the minutes of boards of education or their committees are very valuable, as they show the intermediate level (teachers, principal, and local officials) reacting primarily to external constituencies, but at times to the students, while pursuing their own written and hidden agendas.

You cannot study everything, as Anstead confessed:

> There is also a box of files concerning the various projects to expand the school. Although this is not my sort of history, they might be a very important source to someone who has some idea of what to do with them.
>
> Other sources of information which I have not spent any time on are: mark sheets; floor plans (which I will look at later); records of evening school teachers; janitors' log books (so far janitors are invisible in our history of the school); teachers' salary lists and attendance records. (Anstead's research diary [ARD], October 18, 1983)[1]

We explore some of these issues in the sections which follow.

Official Sources

At the start of our project, we felt that a study of local official records would provide an important framework for understanding Tech. We started with the minutes and annual reports of the board of education. The annual reports allowed us to create a complete, year-by-year outline of the formal courses of study available at the technical school. We soon found that another source—the minutes of the London Board of Education Advisory Industrial Committee (later the Advisory Vocational Committee [ARC and AVC, respectively])—provided much greater detail on Tech than the summaries and reports recorded in the board of education minutes. For the early years, this consists primarily of reports made by Principal Beal, with a few notations of committee motions and votes in response to Beal's suggestions. These minutes contain information on such mundane matters as school maintenance problems or the purchase of supplies, as well as information on the hiring, salaries, and working conditions of teachers and discussions regarding curriculum change in a broad sense. They provide a very extensive look at Beal's ideas and philosophies regarding his school and include rhetorical discussion of the purpose of the school and its various departments. They make fabulous reading and offer insights unavailable from more polished official sources. Covering the period from the origins of the school up until 1971, these papers provide the most important single source on the history of the school.

We could have written a complete, more or less traditional, history of Beal school straight out of these papers. A couple of generations ago, such an approach would have been seen as fitting. But while the minutes do provide a long-term story, they also point out places for more detailed work. We, thus, used the AVC papers as a sort of baseline from which to launch our investigations into other areas.

Sources of useful information may not always be apparent. For instance, we used the personal names of diploma winners in various subjects in order to come up with some approximate figures on gender breakdown. Similarly, we found that a mass of individual student record cards could be used to create aggregate information on the makeup of different courses at the school. Through the use of simple worksheets, we could answer questions on the subjects taken by students of particular courses of study in particular school and calendar years. (For example, what subjects did male students in second-year matriculation take in 1927?)

In support of these findings, we also turned up a number of school "announcements." These pamphlets average about twenty pages each and are dedicated to describing the content and purpose of each course at the school in some detail.

The evolution of school timetables is a promising place to start to build up an historical picture of a school. Other local official sources included individual student timetables showing the accommodations made for special students— for instance, those attending only half days. (Presumably, master timetables existed somewhere for the "typical" students.) A volume entitled *Results of Departmental Examinations* concerned pupils who were to take the provincial examinations for middle and upper schools during the 1930s and 1940s. Each annual report listed the pupils and indicated in which subject(s) they would sit exams. Pay sheets for the school staff during the period of our study listed annual or semi-annual salaries for each teacher but did not mention teachers' subjects or departments.

When we moved further afield, we found official external records including the annual reports and other documents from the Ontario Ministry of Education, as well as the 1913 report of the Royal Commission on Industrial Training and Technical Education. Anstead (1991b) described this source in a brief report:

> The document consists of three sections, each of which provides information of a different type. Parts I and II present the conclusions and recommendations of the Commission. Part III discusses the information found in the Commission's travels through England, Scotland, Ireland, Switzerland, Denmark, Germany, France, and the United States. Part IV summarises the testimony of witnesses interviewed in Canada. The chapters in this section include descriptions of the extent of vocational schooling already in place in each province, as well as outlining any planned developments. The report also provides examples of the thoughts and suggestions of witnesses who appeared at the hearings; the testimony of employers, employees, educators and other interested parties all can be found.

Sources such as this reflect concerns external to the "black box" of the school and as such, may be quite appealing to some researchers. The tendency to look at institutions from outside rather than inside reflects a sense, on the part of many historians, that the facts of institutional history can be established more easily than the facts of a more internal history, especially when commencing the study of an unfamiliar phenomenon. Sources available for institutional history are more abundant and often judged as more reliable than those for more internal, lived experience.

Tracing down information in such documents can lead to interesting excursions. Anstead reported on his work in this regard:

> My specific goal was to determine the role of provincial regulations on the change from the London Industrial School to the London Technical High School. I attempted to find out what the provincial documents had to say. At first I looked at the various Acts of the time which dealt with education, but they all referred to the regulations of the department for the sort of information I needed. Unfortunately, before the 1940s, departmental regulations were not published in a regular, serial, manner. Before that, regulations were published in an irregular manner, and the library apparently had none from the relevant period.
>
> It turned out that I was in a better position than I thought. The reference section of government documents at The University Library had a bibliography of Ontario government publications. This revealed that the regulations published in 1918 and 1920 were, in fact, reprints of the 1914 regulations. By a useful coincidence, the 1914 regulations were the only ones ever included in the annual report of the Minister of Education, and thus were available to me.
>
> On the down side again, the regulations did not actually answer my question. They talked about options which a high school could offer, but did not include any demands about what such a school had to provide. Yet, I am sure that there had to be certain requirements. I think the answer must lie in the letter books of the department, presumably at the Ontario Archives in Toronto. (ARD, November 22, 1991)

It was a disappointing visit:

> I made contact with the Archivist specifically responsible for the Department of Education. Between us, we determined that the material I need is not at the archives. Apparently, the department weeded through its records before transferring them in the early 1950s. Officials eliminated anything thought to be of no historic value. This included all departmental files on specific vocational schools. Thus there is an empty file folder titled "London Technical and Commercial High School." A search of various finding aids and indices for other departmental files turned up nothing which seemed relevant. (ARD, February 6, 1992)

Newspapers

In written form, your chief nonofficial source of evidence is likely to be a local newspaper. Newspaper searches can be exhausting. If you intend to carry one out, get a sense of the task by spending a couple of days reading sample papers to determine the amount of information available and the time it takes to find and summarise it.

Although we carried out a complete newspaper search for the period before 1940, we were unsure of the efficiency of trying to cover the later period. We decided to do a sampling of 1953 papers, a year in the middle of the two periods where we already have scrapbooks (which cover the period up to 1943 and then 1963–1972):

> So far the work is proving tedious and exhausting, but has resulted in some real finds. It takes a long time to scan a whole newspaper when each month fills a complete roll of microfilm, and some months even use two rolls. I have, however, come across a very interesting piece on the opening of the school's new cafeteria—full of information of an "everyday life" sort. I have also found a note on a teacher being punched by a student, and a variety of bits of background information. (ARD, September 2, 1993)

At this point, the reading rate seemed to be roughly nine months in a week's worth of work. It also became clear that most stories on the school came out the day after a meeting of the AVC and reflected issues and information discussed there. The reporter attending the meetings would write two or three small stories which were scattered through the paper:

> It will be interesting to compare these stories to the minutes of the committee. If the minutes are as complete (or more complete) than the newspaper articles, it would mean that the newspaper survey is even less time efficient than it now seems. On the other hand, if there are significant gaps in the minutes, or different interpretations, that will be quite interesting. (ARD, 10, 1993)

As it turned out, we discovered a shortcut:

> Among the things I found in the vault is an index of photos from the *London Free Press*. This notes the subject of any photo taken for the paper, and gives the date published. I plan on using this index as a short-cut through the tedium of reading the whole paper. I have observed that almost every substantive story on the school (aside from those reporting on AVC meetings) includes a photo. I will thus look up each of these pictures and the accompanying story. I think this will give a good coverage of the newspaper's coverage, a relatively small expenditure of time. (ARD, October 18, 1993)

Library clipping files can be useful shortcuts, even if organised in unpromising ways, since even reading every clipping file containing articles from a given newspaper would be easier than reading every page of every issue of the newspaper. The problem instead concerns the coverage of the clippings; in many cases the person building the files only clips articles which deal with "issues" and ignores those which deal with more "ephemeral" subjects. This means that notices of extracurricular activities, sports, or almost anything that does not arouse controversy at the time are ignored.

Scrapbooks kept by concerned individuals tend to be better sources with more complete coverage. An interesting pair of scrapbooks at Beal contains a copy of every advertisement ordered by the school and all press releases printed. These provide full details as far as changes in courses are concerned, as well as some statements of general philosophy and other items of interest.

Other Written Sources

The school environment encourages the production of a variety of other written sources, such as yearbooks. The yearbooks from the Depression and earlier are quite different from those produced today, which are little more than breathless tributes to the graduating class. In the 1930s, Tech's yearbook—the *Tecalogue*—featured articles on a variety of subjects, many of them quite intriguing.

School yearbooks in the period after World War II are different. For the most part, these books consist of pages of class or individual photos, which at least display student appearance and list student activity. You also can use the class photos as a way of getting at course gender statistics (when they disappear from published official sources). And some yearbooks do provide glimpses of everyday life or samples of the student viewpoint.

Another valuable source is a student newspaper. At Beal, *The Word* first appeared in the late 1960s and then resurfaced, after a half decade's lag, in the mid-1970s. Such newspapers can furnish samples of the students' voice. Actually, there are two types of voice: the voice of the "typical" student, captured in "student in the hall" interviews, and the voice of the contributors. During the 1960s, the dominant voice of *Word* contributors was very radical and raises the issue of representation: Were all students this radical, or was the newspaper the place for the school's few radicals to gather? Such questions can be explored in oral interviews.

The scrapbook started by H.B. Beal proved to be a true gold mine. It includes quotes on the philosophy of education and other matters that impressed Beal. The newspaper clippings Beal underlined, and quotations he copied, give more indication of his personal ideology. Thus, the scrapbook tells us something more about the man who was so influential in the establishment and operation of the school. In addition, the scrapbook contains a variety of official school reports on things like enrolment (including gender divisions for a period much earlier than otherwise available), placements, individual withdrawals (with reasons given), and staff.

Student notebooks offer a unique glimpse of classroom life. Our earliest notebook covers a domestic science class for first-year commercial students. The general rules copied by the student say a lot about gender assumptions.

The notebook also includes some handouts from a different class, dealing with the process of interviewing and behaviour on the job.

Note-taking

While identifying sources can be very exciting, the more mundane issue of taking notes determines the ultimate value of what you find. While note-taking technique has to be a personal decision, some general suggestions may help. Historians generally gather data from one source at a time. They only start to organise it thematically later and even then, many still tend to file the notes by source. Thus, instead of having a file called "the school's reputation," you would have "reputation" sections in any number of source-organized files. It might only be at the point of writing that you finally gather all this thematic material together. A decision to generate thematic collections earlier will possibly change your data collection strategy and, thus, influence the final text in unforeseen ways. This is not to say that the other way of working has no influence on the final product, but it does problematise the reasons for the early organisation of material in a long-term study. This raises the historian's traditional reluctance to let theory drive the data collection in obvious ways. And yet, everything we do on a research project is driven by unconscious theoretical assumptions.

In making the notes, you make very conscious decisions about what to include or exclude. Even with the widest possible range of interest, much information will be left unacknowledged. (After all, the point of making notes is to reduce the amount of material that a researcher has to handle.) A basic organising principle might be to include anything which seems to be relevant to the emerging themes of the project. Yet it is the study of the sources (as well as readings in secondary literature and conversations with colleagues) which often leads to the refinement of older themes and the emergence of new ones.

This, then, is something of a chicken-and-egg dilemma: How can you consistently and consciously collect evidence on themes which are yet to emerge? The quick answer is that you cannot, and as new themes come to your attention, you have to broaden your collection patterns or go back over the primary material.

Some types of information have to be collected in other ways. When Anstead undertook an investigation into the course information available on the student record cards, he used worksheets:

> I prepared one sheet for each course in each year. The sheet was divided into columns for each year in the course, and each column was subdivided into gender fields. The rows on the sheet represented the various subjects taught at the school, as listed on the course record forms. I then went through the copies and made a note of every subject

for which a mark was received by each student in each of his or her years of study. This evidence then supported conclusions in terms of gender (the evidence showed different patterns in each course for boys or girls) and status concerns (the data showed how various academic subjects were incorporated into the curriculum of the five different courses offered at Beal. (Anstead, 1994)

As the project expands, you might want to negotiate a narrowing of the focus. An optional step in sifting the huge amount of material in the sources can involve creating thematic summaries. These extracts may or may not become the primary research tools. If they do, the information which did not make it into any extract will probably be ignored.

Interpreting Sources

Probably the most important lesson learned by historians in training is how to address pieces of evidence. What should you accept as a close approximation of past reality? Documents (and other sorts of sources) were created by people. Most of them originated not so that later historians might know what really happened but instead, for contemporary purposes. Sometimes the authors of documents faced constraints in the knowledge they had or time available to check their own sources. Humans make mistakes; they can also exaggerate or misrepresent. This search for biases, subtexts, and mistakes lies at the core of historical inquiry (see Wineburg, 1991). Historians learn to evaluate evidence by seeking likely biases in the authors or in the forms of evidence and then looking for internal consistency or external verification with other sources.

After this, one final screening process occurs, involving the historian's own subjective understanding of the past. If evidence, which passes these practical tests, fits the researcher's mental reconstruction of a particular lived reality, it will be accepted as a likely approximation of reality. If, however, evidence and understanding conflict, the historian must reexamine each. Since different researchers have different understandings of reality, this leaves the door open to disagreement, controversy, and the sort of debate that can keep a discipline invigorated.[2]

We have therefore interrogated evidence from Beal's past by scanning for bias, seeking verification, and applying our own understanding of the past. For instance, the annual reports of the board of education differ from the minutes in that they play down disagreement and disappointments. Yet even the minutes play down some disagreements which are related in the local newspaper. The paper, though, was hardly bias free and in fact, waged a long campaign against Tech. Even without such an obvious bias, newspapers are always subject to the constraints of limited knowledge and deadlines. Newspapers are far from error free; they privilege speed of communication over accuracy of content.

On a big project, it is impossible to do all the research first and then the writing. Instead, research and writing form an intertwined relationship. But writing continually demands access to certain pieces of information. Often, this simply means consulting notes already taken or data already collected, but it will also influence future note-taking or data collection.

The problems and themes addressed in early papers, or in other proposed papers, are always present somewhere in the researcher's thinking. This is not to imply that you should only take notes on things which seem to support your theories, but it does indicate some limitations. The whole process of note-making involves editing an original source for the purposes of future explanatory writing. At times, however, the coincidence of finding important, especially contradictory, evidence causes questions raised in the writing to directly drive the research agenda. A situation of this sort arose from our reading of the minutes of the AVC (an annual report on vocational courses), when we came across some references to provincial participation in the decision to add new courses to the commercial department at Tech. A current working paper we prepared on the commercial course took the premise that the introduction of these courses had been a local initiative. The paper then looked at the results of the presence of these new courses to understand the reason teachers at Beal made the decision to introduce them. If (as this source seemed to imply) the courses were introduced because of pressure from provincial officials, then the whole framework of the paper's argument would have dissolved.

> With this in mind, I adjusted my research calendar and spent several hours with the reports of the Minister of Education for the period 1923–1927. Had this concern not arisen, I was planning to leave the reports until a later date; I would also have started around 1900 and gone straight through to 1940. While my immediate interest was the provincial department's stand on these new commercial courses, I made notes on all the other topics I have followed elsewhere, so that I would not have to return to these volumes at a future date. These reports do not have a lot of information and I will have to find other departmental records at a later time. What I did find was enough to persuade me that provincial officials may have authorised curriculum change and may even have been the first to suggest certain changes, but it was still the teachers and administrators at Beal who made the decision to take advantage of this permission. It was a local decision, if not a local initiative.
>
> Having thus come up with a slightly more nuanced version of my hypothesis for the working paper, I will be setting my research calendar back on track, and returning to the AVC Minutes at the vault. (ARD, July 23, 1991)

Context

A firm rule of historical research states that evidence is useless without context; before anyone can use historical data, they must have a sense of the broader setting. This context consists of at least two dimensions—place and time. For instance, to understand the founding of Tech during the early twentieth century, we have to understand the early twentieth century in general: London, Ontario, and Canada, and the history of education, especially curriculum. Of course, you do not have to conduct intensive primary research in such a wide range of areas. Instead, the secondary literature for each area must be consulted, particularly broad up-to-date surveys and innovative monographs. To find these, you can start with collections of abstracts or indices to relevant journals or electronic databases such as ERIC or Qualidata.

Some researchers would argue that the existing literature furnishes a further context in itself. You need a firm, critical grasp of the literature for several reasons. First, knowing the schools of thought concerning a given subject allows you to place your own research into a theoretical context in a way that readers will grasp quickly—a sort of shortcut. At the same time, knowledge of the literature allows you to ensure that you do not "reinvent the wheel" and makes you aware of the areas of disputed territory where your writing will have to be especially convincing. It can help you to hone your research questions or may suggest further refinements or even unthought-of avenues of interrogation.

The timing of the literature survey is an issue of contention. While one strong school of thought in historical research argues that a researcher should only address primary data after a survey of the secondary literature has led to the framing of a testable, theory-laden hypothesis, more traditional historians find this approach abhorrent, objecting that theory-driven research prevents an open mind. The latter school prefers to start with the evidence and come up with interpretations out of it.

In the Beal project, we find strengths and weaknesses in both approaches. Our own methodology comprises an untidy mix of each, but we suspect that such a mix is not uncommon outside the boundaries of theoretical discourse. Thus, we have approached the evidence only after reading widely in the literature. This reading has allowed us to pose some specific questions, as well as to keep other areas in mind. As we go through the evidence, however, we find our interpretation changing as research questions prove too unrefined and new areas of interest arise. If you take this approach, then, throughout the course of the project you will spend time examining the secondary literature, either in a general way or in an intensive study with a definite goal.

Other intellectual commitments can shape writing and thinking. Membership in formal or informal discussion groups; attendance at conferences, lectures, or workshops; reading outside the project; and discussions with colleagues can all lead you to think again about issues of methodology and interpretation:

> I had an interesting revelation this week which showed me the problems of unconsciously reading the present into the past. I had assumed that the senior matriculation certificate, available only after five years of high school, was the normal route of entrance to the university. On reading books on this period of educational history, however, I found that in the late nineteenth century, it was normal to attend university after completing junior matriculation in four years. The work of fifth year high school and the freshman year at university overlapped and senior matriculants were admitted to the sophomore class. However, senior matriculation was considered a "back-door" route to university for those not able to get in after four years of high school. Obviously that attitude changed during the twentieth century, but I do not know if it was still current in the 1920s and 1930s. This needs to be pinned down. (ARD, November 22, 1991)

CHAPTER THREE

Investigating Quantitative Sources

Of course the most important quantitative source for the Beal project was an almost complete run of student record cards from 1912 (the year the school opened) to 1935. The early cards listed the student's name, address, parent's name, and after 1919, the course in which the student enrolled. After 1927, the cards were much fuller. They included information on religion, date of birth, place of birth, parent's occupation, the student's occupational placement or reason for leaving, as well as a complete set of marks for every class taken.

These cards came and went from the vault in the school. When Ian Dowbiggin made a preliminary collection in approximately 1989, he was able to consult cards from 1912 through to the 1970s. When Anstead returned in 1991, the cards from the last half of the 1930s and the 1940s were missing, apparently having been sent to the main board office for storage on microfiche. By 1993, the situation had changed again:

> The record cards, which we relied on quite heavily for the first part of the project, are gone. Apparently the Board of Education decided to destroy them for the sake of privacy, after recording only the marks students received. This means the loss of valuable socio-economic information, though admittedly the cards for the period after 1940 were much less informative than the earlier cards. Still, had this happened five years earlier, it would have had serious consequences for our study of the 1900–40 period. (ARD, October, 1993)

We also discovered a complementary quantitative source: a few registers giving similar information to the later student cards for different senior classes at the school right after the First World War. This includes things other than attendance, such as address, parent or guardian, parent's occupation, and religion. Although not open to the kind of time line study we could do on the student record cards, the registers do provide snapshots of the more senior grades.

An early report described what Anstead (Anstead, 1994) felt could be done with the student record sources:

> At this point in the study, the best possible use for the cards seems to be an exploration of the relationship between the social class of the student (as measured by the parent's

occupation), the course taken at the school, and the type of job placement experienced by the student after leaving Beal. This analysis would be best handled separately for each gender, since the occupational markets for males and females were so different. In addition, multiple regression analysis can be carried out on other factors—such as birthplace or religion—to search for any causal links to the patterns identified. At a future point, it might be considered useful to plot the students' addresses on a map of London, particularly to determine the representation of students from the East End. (Anstead, 1994)

We decided to use the record cards to study the composition and experience of several cohorts of students. Each set included all those entering a first-year course for the first time in September of a given year in one of these years: 1913–1915, 1919, 1923, 1927, 1931, or 1935. While there was information available for 1912, it posed problems:

> A comparison with the total attendance at the school makes the number of cards collected for 1912 seem too low. Possibly the cards from this year represent only those students who stayed in the school for two or more years. In other words, maybe in the first year, records for students who left were discarded. (ARD, June 27, 1991)

Not every cohort received equally detailed treatment. For some, the information collected included information on the student's school career, such as years passed or failed and any transfers to other departments; the marks assigned for conduct and attendance; the average grade received in the third term of the school year; and the outcome of the school year (for example, pass, fail, quit while failing, quit for job, illness). These attendance and conduct marks seemed to promise to tell us something about student action and could be compared to socioeconomic factors.

Decisions of this nature have to be made on the spot, as data collection proceeds:

> I spent Friday and Monday in the vaults at Beal. The student record cards for 1927–35 are stored together in two drawers there. They are sorted alphabetically, but not by year. In verifying Dowbiggin's cards and adding my own, I have had to decide what students I really want represented. It turns out that I am creating three related collections of cards from 1927. The major collection will be the students who entered first year of one of the general courses in 1927 (commercial, technical or matriculation).... The other collections feature those entering the special commercial course for the first time in 1927 and those going to special technical courses with no previous tech school record.... For the first two groups (1927 general entrants and special commercial), I am adding information on school career, outcome in 1927 and marks for attendance, conduct and academic average. On all cards I am adding the exact class attended, which allows me to make the distinction between the various groups of students noted above. (ARD, May, 1991)

Indeed, the spotting of a trend or discrepancy can happen at the spur of the moment and lead to changes in strategy:

> I want to go through all the matriculation course students in the file and determine the extent to which they completed their course. I have a sense from reading the cards, that less than ten per cent actually graduated with credentials opening their way to higher education. I think I will set up a separate collection for this group, in a new data base. (ARD, June 3, 1991)

Some researchers accept quantifiable data such as student record cards at face value, arguing that no reason exists for bias, but this is a naive, if convenient, rationalisation. In our case, for instance, the possibility exists that students tended to report a more "respectable" parental occupation or a more successful placement. (Of course, some researchers would argue that an expressed occupation, by revealing personal class identification, tells us more about an individual than an actual occupation would.) Outright errors are also possible.

A research team can check some of these things. You can compare listed occupations with the manuscript census (if available) or with local directories and tax rolls.

We supplemented the record cards from the first decade in the history of the school by reference to contemporary directories. Here though, one immediately encounters the problem of linkage between records. For instance, when can you be reasonably certain that the parent of a student and a person mentioned in a directory are the same individual?

To address this issue, you need to establish a series of criteria. This process may start as an unconscious one but quickly surfaces when faced with unclear cases. Obviously, you can feel confident in assuming a link when parental name and address match exactly with information in the directory. In those cases where the parent's name did not appear in the directory at that address, or at all, or where the name appeared but without any occupation listed, you have to take other steps:

> The first step I took involved looking up the address in the street directory, which listed the household head for each address. In cases where the household head had the same surname as the parent from the student card, I determined the occupation of the household head and used it as the parental occupation. This strategy was used chiefly in cases where a female parent was listed on the student card. Of course, in cases where the female parent did have an occupation listed in the directory, that became the parental occupation on the card. Most of the cards left were put aside for the search of the next directory. Thus up to this point, all the cards with information on parental address added had matched both address and surname. In a very few cases, I added information to cards without a matching address. I did this only in cases where

the parental name (first name, middle name or initial where known, and last name) matched exactly one in the directory, and where the name was somewhat unusual. In general, this applied to people with non-British first or last names, though some people with British surnames did have very rare first names. (ARD, August 9, 1991)

In the end, we found an occupation for the parent or household head for at least 80 percent of the cards. Of the remainder, about one half could not be linked because of inadequate address information on the student cards.

The interpretation of data of this sort usually involves the creation of data banks—coded bundles of information which can be manipulated by statistical software. Some items are fairly straightforward; coding categories for gender, course, age, or marks involve little decision making. Variables such as socioeconomic standing, however, can be trickier and represent a key methodological decision, which may be contested by your readers:

> I am at the point where I want to start analysis of the data, but to do so requires some aggregation of occupational titles into categories, presumably based on some theory of social class. We decided to define occupational categories which will be useful in the long run, and which we do not see as necessarily proxies for class. At present we see London's class system consisting of three groups: a tiny elite, a middle class and a working class. None of these groups are defined by occupation alone, though occupation serves as a constraint.... We decided to create seven working categories for the organisation of occupational titles. These categories are: professionals; teachers; other non-manual; skilled manual; unskilled manual; farmers; and not classified. This is a flexible system, since these categories can be aggregated easily. The correspondence with class goes as follows. The elite consists of the wealthiest families, and may be drawn from any of the first four categories (since a factory owner may still refer to himself by a craft title).
>
> The middle class includes all other non-manual workers, and some skilled manual workers. The working class consists of the remainder of skilled manual workers, and all the unskilled. Farmers and others do not correspond to a specific class. (ARD, August 17, 1991)

Additional problems face any study of the young:

> The grouping of occupational titles into broad categories for the placement positions poses some problems. Certain jobs, which are just jobs for adolescents, seem to say little about student life chances. In other words, I'm not sure that the first job many students take, on leaving high school, has any effect on their career. I am thinking of those who become "messengers," "errand boys," "copy boys," "stock boys," "paper boys" or "pin boys." At present, I have set up the codes so that students going to these positions are not classified, while students who go to adult positions are. (ARD, April 16, 1991)

The use of the resultant statistics depends on your theoretical approach and methodological orientation. We did do some multiple regression analysis on our data cohorts but decided instead to publish much simpler, but more robust, forms of analysis.

Conclusion

Finding, examining, and using written sources is one of the most important undertakings in the preparation of any school history. Yet it is not always enough—oral and visual sources should not be overlooked.

CHAPTER FOUR

Collecting Oral Sources

Introduction

Oral evidence provides a unique perspective on any school's history. An interview subject can provide information not available in written records and answer specific research questions. The techniques of the interview itself are a crucial component of data collection of oral sources. Mishler (1986) has provided a valuable guide to research interviewing, and Kvale and Brinkmann (2009) have provided significant reminders of the importance of power and perception in the interview process. In the interview, you can find out something of what went on behind closed doors—whether those doors led to a boardroom or a classroom. This benefit comes with disclaimers, though: you have to consider the influence of the interview itself—the setting, the personal interplay—on the construction of the new source document, and you must assess the perspectives, biases, and partial recall of the interviewee.

Finding People

Obviously, the first thing you need when starting an oral history is someone to interview, and there are at least three ways you can come up with a list of possible subjects. The first method is to use your personal contacts and their networks. This may include people whom you know for one reason or another, and who coincidentally went to the school, or people you meet while working on the project. Sometimes your interview subjects themselves will phone a friend or acquaintance to introduce them to you.

The second way is to make public requests for volunteers. In January 1992, we sent a letter for publication in the local paper asking for oral witnesses for the first part (1912–1940) of our study. It read,

```
Sir,

We would like to seek help from your readers. We are
presently engaged in a study of curriculum change which
```

focuses on the history of Beal Secondary School from its founding up until 1940. Having examined all the official records from the school and the government, we have redrawn part of the picture, but there are still some cloudy areas.

In particular, we do not have a clear view of what actually went on in the classroom. Thus we are hoping to interview some of the people who were involved with the school in this period, or borrow private notebooks or other papers which might throw some light on classroom life at the time.

We would like to hear from anyone who was a student or teacher at the "London Industrial School," the "London Technical and Commercial High School," or the "H.B. Beal Technical and Commercial High School" at any time from its founding until the start of the Second World War. Please call us at 661-3845 between 9:00 a.m. and 3:00 p.m., Monday to Friday. We will set up an interview date at a time and place convenient for you.

In addition, we are also quite interested in any informal records of the school experience at "Tech." We would greatly appreciate the loan of any school notebooks, or any other personal papers (such as diaries or letters) which deal with school life. If you have kept or inherited notebooks or other relevant papers, please give us a call at the number above. While we are interested in this sort of valuable information from the whole period under review, we aim this appeal particularly at the children and grandchildren of the teachers and students who were at the school in its very earliest days, during the First World War.

Thank you for your help.

The response to the letter was quite exciting. Altogether, some thirty-five people phoned in; roughly two dozen were former students while the others had some other contribution to make. The former students represented a range of ages, from those who attended in the early 1920s to others in the late 1930s. Unfortunately, this did not produce a cross section of gender by courses. With the exception of one woman (who took nursing and dietetics), the respondents were either male technical students or female commercial students.

The third approach can fill in some of the gaps of representation; it involves the use of "cold call" sources, that is, lists of former students or teachers who do not know you and have not expressed interest in the project as yet. This might include names given you by former interviewees or lists from other sources.

We used a list of former students (with graduating year) who attended the school's seventy-fifth anniversary in 1987 as our "cold call" source. We started by taking this compilation and paring it down to a shorter list including two to four members of each graduating class, including both genders. The people on this shorter list all lived in London or the surrounding area and according to the phone book, were at the same address they were at in 1987. (There seemed little point in trying to follow up addresses which had changed in the intervening five years.) Obviously, this was not a random selection of former Beal students. It included only those people interested enough in their school to attend the celebrations (and, thus, probably underrepresented any dissident view). It also represented only those people who stayed in the London area, who had a stable address, and who could afford a telephone.

Using all three of these approaches, we ended up interviewing fifty-three people. We managed to get a fairly equal representation of genders, of teachers and students, and of the decades in the school's history. We also obtained a proportional representation of courses taken or taught.

You can contact prospective interview subjects by phone, but a letter gives them more time to reflect and can include an invitation to contact you if they are interested. A follow-up phone call a week or so later is usually necessary, especially if the number of responses seems very low. Once started this way, you can pursue the networks of these people to reach other former students or teachers (called "snowball" sampling by some), including those with a distinctive view of the institution. It is hard to gauge the success you will have:

> I am a bit surprised at how successful I have been with requesting their cooperation. I suppose I always felt that most retired people would enjoy sharing their memories, but I did not expect that the same would be true of people my own age. So far, though, only one person has said "no" and he was in the first group. (ARD, March 2, 1994)

Conducting the Interview

The amount of time needed for an interview will vary from researcher to researcher, depending on methodology, but it will also be very different from subject to subject. A maximum of three appointments per day (one in the morning, one in the afternoon, and one in the evening) means you do not need to rush anyone, leave a fruitful interview before the speaker is done, or arrive late.

An interview should have some collaborative elements; give each subject a chance to set the procedural rules for the interview. Some will want a question-and-answer format and will provide answers which are informative and to the point. Although the interview might be short, it will contain a lot of information. Our preferred approach involved devoting the first segment of the interview to the memories of the subject with little prompting at all. Most of the people you interview will have spent some time thinking about the school in the time since contact. Ask them to share those thoughts. Some like to make notes in advance—it is always a good idea to ask about this and then start with a discussion of them. You may find other people participating in the interview, either spouses and relatives who just happen to have memories of the school or the context or friends from school specifically invited over (with or without your knowledge) to join the discussion.

The personalities and characteristics of the interviewer or team will have an impact on the interview as conversation. Interviews which cross lines of gender, ethnicity, or age-group may give a different result from those which do not. If one of the interviewers shares some characteristics with the subject, it might put him or her at ease and, thus, encourage greater participation in the interview process.

Despite your best efforts, some interviews will seem of little worth. Some people cannot stay on topic in their reminiscences. Despite any number of attempts to steer them back to the matter at hand, they will talk about the present or totally unconnected past experiences. Even these interviews can produce useful information—it just takes more work to find it. Every interview of this sort which we conducted still provided at least one or two pieces of information which added immeasurably to the whole picture.

Information

There are at least three types of information which can be found in an interview, depending on your own interests: first, behind-the-scenes explanation of specific events; second, day-to-day detail of lived experience; and third, information reflecting the constructed memory of an institution.

For the first sort of information, teachers and administrators tend to be a preferred source. Even when dealing with a secondary school like Beal, we found that none of the students were aware of any tensions or conflict at the staff level. They tended to think of the principal not as an actor pursuing personal or institutional goals but purely in terms of his responsibility for discipline. So, while these interviews are tremendously helpful in dealing with some types of questions, they leave others completely unanswered.

You can use the aggregate impressions of a large number of interviews to evolve a description of the day-to-day educational experience. (This may mean discarding any memories that seem atypical or influenced by events or factors not common to all students.) For the most part, it is an incremental process; though no single interview will give you confidence in a mental reconstruction of the past, the mosaic of new detail and repeated patterns you will find will allow you that confidence. After conducting the first fifteen interviews, Anstead started to feel that he had a fairly accurate picture of classroom life in the school between the wars:

> I have images of the teaching styles of many different teachers; I can visualize the sort of projects technical students undertook; I can imagine what the atmosphere in class, or in the halls, was like. (ARD, March 23, 1992)

But to reach this level of confidence, it was necessary to undertake these multiple interview sessions.

On the other hand, you may be very interested in the oral testimony of individuals as individuals. In most interviews, the schooling experience is presented in rosy tones. In the case of Beal, the main themes of this sort of interpretation were that students were disciplined and showed respect for their teachers; that every teacher—without exception—was good, and many went beyond the call of duty; and that all students, whatever their socioeconomic background, were treated the same. Frequent comparisons to the present system of education were made, with many negative comments about the latter.

This positive view of their school days may be the result of four factors. First, the selection process: Those people who most enjoyed or valued their school experience were most likely to answer our advertisement. The second factor is related to the way memories are stored. Most long-term memories are stored as analysed pieces of information, that is, the brain first looks for patterns, or links to older information, before storing a memory. When the memory is invoked, the accompanying analysis comes with it. However, at the time of childhood memory storage, the individual probably has little in the way of a critical mind. When childhood memories are retrieved, they do not come with critical analytical interpretations. Such interpretations only arise when the subject decides to confront his or her memories in light of later experience. Third, many people see choices made in high school as determining their whole career. Challenging the legitimacy of the educational experience thus translates as challenging the whole life experience, which most people are unwilling to do. Finally, you cannot dismiss the positive out of hand; there is probably some truth behind the platitudes.

An alternative type of interview is rare. We found a few former students from the interwar period who presented more critical views of their past. These students still had a generally positive view of Tech, and described their school days as the "best of times." Yet they were also willing to say that certain teachers were not very good. They also pointed to some types of discrimination either in the school or on the part of outsiders describing the school. For the later period, this became more common, with some students flatly condemning the school, and with even those who said they liked it willing to report on some of the darker sides—like the school's underclass reputation, the use of drugs and the like (ARD, February 21, 1994).

Life History

The construction of life histories involves a series of lengthy interviews in which the subject recounts his or her life story (Denzin, 1989, Goodson & Sikes, 2001; Plummer, 2001). The resultant transcripts and accounts are then presented to the subjects for revision, editing, or correction. When placed in a context including theoretical understandings and a sociohistorical description of the time and place, each life history becomes a story of action (as described by the subject) within a framework of structures (as identified by both the researcher and the subject). They pay attention to the whole life experience, attempting to describe what it was like to live these people's lives—what it was like to take their place in school, at work, or in society—and how they interpreted their social and cultural surroundings.

Life history interviews should be conducted in a collaborative way. You should encourage each subject to seize control of the interview process and determine the direction of inquiry. Your questions will probe the topics chosen by the subject, and new directions will only be introduced through negotiation.

In the periods between interviews, you will prepare transcripts or drafts of the life history. As you start to produce a life history, you will bring it to the subject for revision or new contributions. You might also raise contextual or theoretical concerns and suggestions with the subject, who will decide whether or not to pursue them. Any such material included within a life history will also have to be cleared by the subject.

Bias and Interpretation

Issues of bias lie at the heart of oral history methodology; its most obvious form is bias on the part of the interview subject. Individual memories can be coloured by later experiences or can be simply mistaken. Corroboration of material gathered in this way depends on a triangulation process chiefly involving external documentary sources.

If your aim is to produce a triangulated life history, this material should be included, as long as the subject agrees to it. Should this external research turn up something which seems to contradict the subject's story, then you have to raise it at the next meeting. On the other hand, if you are more interested in recounting the narrative someone tells of their life, the contextual material could be reserved for an external commentary.

A concrete example of the sort of dilemma we faced when we moved into the oral testimony stage of the project arose during a conversation with one of the teachers at Beal. When Anstead mentioned the oral interviews that had already been carried out for the project, this teacher was quite outspoken in his opinion that one of our informants was not a "typical" teacher. He said that this teacher was in fact heartily disliked by both staff and students, due to certain autocratic tendencies (ARD, October 21, 1991). This raises some issues about the associated oral testimony. Should evidence of behaviour deemed inappropriate today alter our reading of the oral testimony from an earlier period? Is it possible that teachers placed in such a defensive position at the end of a long career might present their testimony as a self-serving illustration of their ultimate good sense? More generally, is there such a thing as a "typical" teacher, and should we seek them out?

Another form of bias derives from the process itself. Thinking of interviews in terms of verification of the facts and interpretations presented equates them with other sorts of historical data. But an interview is more than just a recital of the relevant facts by an informed insider. Instead, an interview is a unique communications event in which all traditional rules of conversation are fractured. As researcher and subject interact, they create a document which summarizes, describes, and details things that the subject might not discuss in such ways. The interviewer constructs a discourse as the interview proceeds. In interviewing, you should always try to let the subject lead the discussion as much as possible. Yet at some time, you will take over each interview. You will ask for clarification, look for verification of interpretations of their words, or seek to pursue—or avoid—particular topics. Thus, you are taking an important role in the construction of the account, urging the subjects to express themselves in ways they had never intended to. This is what an oral historian does and there is nothing wrong with it, as long as you accept that your presence (as well as the presence of tape recorders and any witnesses, such as a spouse) can change the subject's presentation of the past. In our own work, we tried to control some of this bias by asking a colleague to attend some of the interviews and even take the dominant role on a couple of occasions.

In some ways the role of the interviewer parallels that of the author (rather than the reader) of a historical document. Interviewing surviving teachers and students involves the researchers directly in the creation of new sources of historical evidence. Most supporters answer concerns about this by saying that a well-trained practitioner would avoid any obvious contamination of the evidence, though absolutely value-free interviewing is impossible. At the core of this defence of oral history is the argument that all the concerns raised about verification could equally be raised about more traditional sources, and while the role of the interviewer/historian is unique, so is the ability to directly question a historical source.

At times even false information can have its uses:

> One of the interesting titbits that has arisen concerns a sort of "urban myth" in the school. I had a student from the 1960s describe how some of the boys at the school dangled Mr. Fallona out the third story windows at the school. Yet I also heard exactly the same story from one of the pre-war students a couple of years ago. I checked with a couple other interviewees, who also reported hearing this sort of vague story. I think there is something important here—a part of the school's individual culture. (ARD, February 21, 1994)

Ethical Issues

While there is a balance of power in the oral history relationship—the interviewee has information the researcher needs, but the researcher has the ability to shape and use the material once delivered—the ethical onus is on the latter. A number of ethical issues impinge on the use of oral evidence, with the first priority being informed consent. You need to provide each subject with a full consent form, outlining the rights and obligations of both parties, and it must be delivered with a full explanation of your project and dissemination plans. The oppressiveness of these ethical and legal necessities can sometimes lead to obstacles:

> When I brought out the consent form, [the interview subject] was reluctant to sign. I left the form with him, and returned on Thursday. At that point I realized that his hesitancy sprang from his memories of teaching days. He felt that some of the lighter anecdotes might cast some disrespect on the principal at the time. Thus we added a condition to the consent form, granting his permission for use of the material which covered the period up to 1940, but not later. (ARD, February 24, 1992)

In general the researcher has to be willing to accede to any request from the interviewee. Although historical work generally uses real names, rather than the pseudonyms of much social science work, some of your contacts may not want their full name used. You have to agree. On occasion, a person might be uncomfortable about the use of the tape recorder, even if you have already mentioned it when setting up the meeting. In such cases, your only option is to make field notes and write down as full a report of the interview as possible immediately afterwards.

Life history work magnifies these concerns. As potential subjects for this sort of investigation are located, you have to be wary of exerting pressure to make them open up something so personal as the recounting of their lives to public perusal and use. You need to search for people who want to tell their stories. Finally, the life history, once written, should only be used with the full agreement of the subject.

Transcription

Transcribing an interview is a key stage in any project. For purposes of research, a verbatim transcript must include all the false starts, hesitations, and nonverbal components of a real conversation. (To avoid embarrassing your subjects, however, you will need to edit these out of any published quotes.) No matter how precise your final transcript is, transcription remains a process of translation. And, as in all translations, something is lost. A key aim has to be to reduce the loss to a minimum.

Why then would you want to transcribe oral encounters? The answer is that many researchers find transcripts more efficient than working with a tape. A transcript can be copied for multiple researchers, can be searched quickly (especially if you load it into a qualitative text databank), and can serve as a source for cut-and-paste quotes. Above all, written data is more amenable to word processing than is un-transcribed oral data.

It is not always clear, however, that the benefits of "efficiency" justify the time involved in making a transcription or excuse the loss of sensitivity (or of meaning) which occurs in translation. It seems possible that an alternative methodology, comprising repeated listenings to the tape recording of an interview, consultation with field notes, and the creation of a simple but robust index to the interview, would serve these purposes just as well—at a lower cost in time and in knowledge lost. Only the quotations to be included in published papers then need to undergo the indignity of transcription. The choice is, again, up to you.

Conclusion

Oral history takes many forms and the extended bibliography lists a number of examples. It can provide information which fills in the gaps in the stories of events. It can also serve to build up a brick-by-brick reconstruction of everyday life at a particular time. Among the most striking forms are the self-delivered life story and the researcher's construction of triangulated life histories. While both of these are obviously "stories," so, in fact, are all the histories you might try to tell.

SECTION TWO

CHAPTER FIVE

Developing a Narrative Overview

In studying the life of a school, an important task is to develop a historical narrative of the school's evolution. In particular, this means scrutinising patterns of stability and change. The historian's craft is to produce an account which is grounded in historical evidence, takes a form that cuts through complexities and irrelevancies, and attempts to cast meaningful light on past human behaviour and experience (see McCulloch & Richardson, 2000).

History can be an attempt to present a usable past. Any present-day attempt to promote curriculum stability or curriculum change or more broadly, school reform, demands an understanding of history; reformers must first consult the record of success and failure in the past.

Although, when we use the word *history* we instinctively think of the past, this is an error, for history is actually a bridge connecting the past with the present and pointing the road to the future (Nevins, 1938, p. 14).

Of course, we should not overstate continuities in the face of complexities, but exploring the links between past, present, and future remains a vital task.

The Nature of Narratives

The most traditional approach to the history of an institution is one which features a long narrative overview. The story of the school is laid out as the story of progress or less often, conflict, through the decades. Aside from principals and board officials, few individuals appear. It is almost as though the school were animate and this was its life story. Highlights are typically the expansion of the physical plant, the introduction of new programs and things that made the school stand out from others of its kind—paralleling the stories of physical growth, intellectual development, and individual personality which mark out our own personal biographies.

Choosing this sort of approach means you avoid getting caught up in events or specific individuals but changes in that a linear study of unproblematic developments is presented without sufficient attention to discontinuities and turning points. Gaps in sources that describe specific phenomena can be papered over, which means descriptive histories generally lack voices describing experience in a subjective way and often, discussions of intentions. It is possible to write a narrative of almost anything, but it is much more difficult to prove deep and meaningful connections.

It is important to make your mind as open as possible, but

> if history became impartial in the sense of lacking conviction it would be a poor affair. Historians must judge evidence, not prejudge it. Conviction comes during research, not before it. (Nevins, 1938, pp. 57–58)

The study of the history of education has tended to take an "external" view of curriculum, focusing on political and administrative contexts and on general movements in education and schooling. The reasons for the dominance of "Acts and Facts" history of education are numerous. Perhaps most important was the carryover from the general mode of historical scholarship at the time that history of education courses were first devised. History as a discipline in the universities was growing quite rapidly at this time and was primarily concerned with national, constitutional, and political matters told in a narrative manner (Berger, 1986; R. Davis, 1981; Higham, 1965). Moreover, in the educational domain itself, it was a time when the organisation, administration, and alteration of educational structures and systems seemed at the heart of attempts to improve schooling.

Though the specific social and political contexts of nineteenth-century Britain and North America contributed to this pattern, so did the associated range of documentary evidence on which history has to build its interpretations, which often relate to central government regulations, edicts, or commissions on education and curriculum. For the historian, the effects of contemporary selection and associated documentation are often conclusive:

> To some extent, the selection begins within the period itself; from the whole body of activities, certain things are selected for value and emphasis. In general this selection will reflect the organisation of the period as a whole, though this does not mean that the values and emphases will later be confirmed. We see this clearly enough in the case of past periods, but we never really believe it about our own. (Williams, 1961, p. 67)

Historians of education, who search out new areas of study, therefore, often collide with the intractable selections of past periods (Andrews, 1983). The "selective tradition" joins with contemporary definitions of the relative importance of different types of historical problems to maintain history of education as a discipline which takes an external approach to schools.

This is a long way from curriculum as transacted at the level of the classroom. Histories of education which fail to analyse the internal nature of schooling merely accept the school as a "black box," unopened and unanalysed, ignoring the vast potential for internal variety and change. It is within schools and in particular, within classrooms, where the reality of curriculum delivery is negotiated; yet this is the one forum most neglected by historians of education. A few leaders in the field have pointed to this omission. Chad Gaffield (1986) called on Canadian historians of education to go "back to school," and described the lack of any study of the classroom as "a major weakness in the current historiography of education" (p. 183). According to Harold Silver (1992), in history of education as currently practised, "There are no classrooms, no children, no teaching, no learning" (p. 104). Silver concluded, "We have been writing the history of educational contexts, not of education" (p. 107).

Despite the foregoing, characterising history of education in the past as predominantly "Acts and Facts" is less than fair; as with any subject, history of education has not been, and is not, monolithic. In the last quarter century, a growing literature, particularly from the United States, has drawn inspiration from catalytic changes in mainstream history. Economic and social history have grown rapidly since the interwar years; oral history and feminist history have developed to try to exhume the "invisible armies" suppressed by selective traditions; and the work of Hobsbawm (1959/1965), Thompson (1968), Genovese (1974), Smith-Rosenberg (1985), and many others illustrates how the lived experiences in our culture can be reconstructed by historians. Since 1970 or so, historians of education have carved out a professional niche for themselves in the academic field of mainstream history. They have linked up with the concerns of the dynamic social historians, leading to useful studies of education in terms of class, gender, ethnicity, and the family (Aldrich, 1987; Gaffield, 1986; Harrigan, 1986; Wilson, 1984, 1990).

You have to set issues in the broadest context and reflect on changing economic and social relations. Thus, our theory for the founding of Tech was that nationalism, social efficiency, reform, and industrial needs all led to try for vocationalism, with the middle-class capitalist response of stratification. This amalgam, then, ran into local educators like Beal with their own ideas (ARD, January 22, 1991). All the potential organizing principles could add up to chaos. In other words, do you tell the story of a period of a division or department in the school or instead, of a level of understanding? Obviously, you will want to include all of these possibilities as points of discussion, but only one story can be told as a unified one; the others have to appear and reappear as they intersect the "master narrative."

The most important part is not analysis of data but creation of a broad interpretation (Nevins, 1938, p. 262). A pile of facts is not history (Nevins, 1938, p. 299):

> History which lacks a thesis is a body lacking a skeleton—it is invertebrate. It may contain exhaustive research, may be striking in detail, may throw new light into dark places, but its total effect will be limp. (Nevins, 1938, p. 295)

A master narrative depends on a single, broad, organizing theme. In our case, we organized drafts around

> the intermediary and independent role of the school's teachers, as they seek to answer the demands and criticisms of external constituencies, pursue their own personal and professional interests, and still interact with their students (who have their own agendas). (ARD, August 9, 1993)

Telling the narrative story involves gathering and weighing evidence, then using inductive logic and hypotheses to produce provisional generalizations which have to be tested through a search for new data (Nevins, 1938, p. 29).

The telling of narrative stories is an artful process in which you must use richness of context to set up the description of action and consequence (O. Davis, 1991, pp. 78–79)

History has to be buttressed by the use of primary evidence.

Avoid presentism.

The meanings presented in such a story are the artful interpretations of you as author. History does not provide clear and agreed meanings, and very few generally agreed facts, so your interpretation of the historian has always to be mindful that new facts may be discovered or a "more likely rendering" of the past may subsequently be produced (O. Davis, 1991, p. 79):

> The entire vitality and interest of history depends upon the fact that universally acceptable summaries are impossible. (Nevins, 1938, p. 228)

> The simple fact is that few stories are available of curriculum practice in particular schools undertaken by particular individuals during particular times. (O. Davis, 1991, p. 82)

> History is never above the melee. It is not allowed to be neutral, but forced to enlist in every army. (Nevins, 1938, p. 23)

> As the users of curriculum documents see only the present-day relevance, they routinely discard them when the next modification arrives. (O. Davis, 1991, p. 83)

The broad compass of a typical narrative can lead to information overload. For instance, in discussing the emergence of vocationalism as a social movement in London, we first asked these questions: Who was behind it? Why? Who spoke for them? Why this time period? Where did the idea come from? How did it affect students? Why London? How did London fit the provincial or national picture? What was the role of capital, workers, teachers, children, politicians, parents, the state? Did it reflect market versus political tension? What was the underlying power (ARD, January 7, 1991)?

The story of a school has to be organized somehow. At one time, we were thinking in terms of historical eras and subject departments as the master organizing principles. We also planned to use specific subject departments as case studies for understanding larger administrative divisions (technical studies, for instance) in the postwar period. Topics would include:

> The school's origins; histories of the main curricular divisions: technical, commercial, and academic; the history of the art program; a portrayal of the student experience (although this might be scattered through other chapters too). (ARD, August 9, 1993)

This organization would be replicated for two periods: 1912–1940 and 1940–1980. Each chapter would then look at the history of the school from three viewpoints—the external context (both broad and narrow), the actions and reactions of the teaching staff, and the nature of everyday classroom and school life (ARD, December 7, 1993).

Example: Education for Efficiency— The History of an Innovative School

The story of Beal is the story of innovation: in tune with the times. The story can be broken down into eight periods, during most of which school staff experimented with new curriculum forms in light of changing social and economic situations. The choice of a history constructed around "periods" is one of a number of options open to the historian; other genres are to organise the text around thematic clusters or to choose one overriding theme and follow its emergence and trajectory. For us, the choice of periods grew from our analysis of the archives from people's testimonies.

The first period in the school's history can be defined as lasting from its founding in 1912 to the early 1920s. At the turn of the century, vocationalism appeared as the education plank in the new social efficiency platform (Cremin, 1961; Kantor, 1988; Kliebard, 1986; Stamp, 1970). The idea that business approaches based on scientific rationality could manage the social world as efficiently as the economic one was a powerful message in the cultural milieu. Efficient schools were those which fit students for their future lives in the workplace—students who would be trained for roles needed in the local economy, without any additions. The main mechanism involved streamlining students into courses based on their future occupations.

In Ontario, capitalists supported technical education which would train future workers without investing them with liberal learning. Educational reformers joined them but were interested in fewer divisions between the types of education in terms of status. Organized labour agreed with the latter group. The result was the Industrial Education Act of 1911.

In London, Herbert Benson Beal emerged as the chief advocate for social efficiency through vocationalism. In 1912, the city's board of education agreed to establish the London Industrial School as a terminal vocational secondary school (Anstead Report Notes, December 5, 1911. Beal was named principal of London Industrial School (established 1912) and was to operate under the supervision of an advisory committee made up of trustees from the board of education and representatives of employers and employees.

In the new school, first opened in a few basement rooms in an aging elementary school, Beal sought to emphasize practical training, with academic subjects taught in ways related to the practical side. He took many of his cues in curriculum setting from local employers and workers. For the first few years, the school offered little in the way of traditional structure. Students were separated by gender but not by grade or major. Subject boundaries remained vague. While commercial art was added to the curriculum, no university preparation courses were offered.

By the time the school moved into its own permanent building during the 1918–1919 school year, this early, experimental phase had ended. Principal Beal found that his innovative approach tended to alienate more conservative sources of money and status, as well as the parents of prospective students. To gain all these resources, he needed to turn his school into a recognized high school (AVC, 1918, p. 114). With this in mind, the school introduced the traditional framework of grades, subjects, and courses, as well as a new university preparation course. In late 1919, the "London Industrial and Art School" became the "London Technical High School."

The second period, the 1920s, was a period when many social definitions were undergoing challenge. This included vocational definitions, as clerical work slipped down the ladder and skilled technical work came to be more highly valued and rewarded.

The school saw a fundamental alteration, with the transfer of the commercial program from the city's academic secondary school (causing a name change to the "London Technical and Commercial High School," but still known locally as Tech). By the middle of the decade, commercial students could choose between a three-year general course (with an option to leave after two years), a one-year special course for senior students and graduates, or a "Special Business Course for Boys" which trained young men for positions offering "ample opportunity for advancement" (AVC, 1927, p. 7; 1928, p. 3).

Principal Beal continued to emphasize his commitment to employer participation in curriculum making, while challenging the existing emphasis on liberal education aimed at the professions. He argued that his school was preparing students efficiently for success in productive occupations. Thus, it was with the advice of a committee of local representatives that the school established a printing course in 1924 (AVC, 1924, p. 36), adding it to a curriculum which featured woodworking, machine shop, electricity, building construction, and drafting—generally taught in big workshops housing two classes with two different teachers. Despite some opposition, the local board and provincial department funded the building of an expansion in 1928, which brought gymnasium and auditorium facilities to the school. Before that, the only areas for physical training were a cinder court between wings of the school or a basement room full of pipes (H. Cull, interview; N. Hopkins, interview). With the addition, the school could offer its first regular extracurricular activities, such as sports, dances, and shows.

Moral panic caused by the changing value of work meant Beal and his school underwent another series of newspaper attacks in 1923–1924. Charging it with being too expensive, too poorly used, and offering poor education, opponents tried to have Tech converted into a comprehensive high school serving all the students from the city's East End (*London Free Press* [*LFP*], December 29, 1923 to February 8, 1924).

The coming of the Depression altered conditions for Tech students, though a few left early to try to earn some money for their families, many stayed in school longer since they knew there were no jobs to be found upon graduation. With financial constraints on their students and funding scarce, teachers at Tech did not introduce much curriculum change during the ten years of hardship, though at one point in the 1930s, the third year of the girls' technical course was eliminated and replaced with a special, one-year nursing and dietician course (Spence, interview). The school continued to provide technical subjects (distinct for each gender), commercial programs, and art. In contrast to later years, all students faced large homework loads and regular exams.

With the retention of so many students and the inability of the school board to afford a building program, Tech became extremely crowded. In response, Principal Beal introduced a "staggered" system of classes in September 1933, with students attending eight out of twelve periods during the school day—some coming early, some leaving late, and some having long lunch hours (London Board of Education, 1933, pp. 245–246; 1934, p. 208; London Technical and Commercial High School, 1934).

With students lacking after-school jobs, and no money for other forms of leisure, and with teachers unable to innovate in the classroom, school extracurricular activities became especially vibrant during the Depression.

Besides sports teams, the orchestra, and the usual clubs, Tech produced an annual school show involving hundreds of students. The show ran for several nights each spring, attracting sell-out crowds.

The next period in the school's history coincides with the massive social and economic changes wrought by Canada's participation in World War II. The Second World War altered the conditions of schooling at Beal in several ways beyond the absence of staff and older students who left to do war work or serve in the armed services. Representing an important capital investment in technical training equipment, the school building came to be used more and more as a way of filling the ranks of skilled industrial workers needed for war industry.

From the summer of 1940 through to the start of 1945, the school offered "war emergency courses," under the Dominion-Provincial youth training program, to train men in war-related work (AVC, April 10, 1940; January 11, 1945). The school also ran specialist courses, including a three-month training program for aeroplane mechanics hired by a massive local plant. The numbers in this course were so great that it had to be run in an old factory building. In addition, the school ran courses for the army and air force in a variety of areas, such as cooking or radio telegraphy. The war also caused the breaking of a gender barrier at Beal, with the first courses opened to women in the areas of motor mechanics and machine shop. The school building itself came to run on a 24-hour basis. Besides regular day and evening classes, the board of education added midnight classes in technical subjects.

Once the war's expected duration became apparent, school and board administrators undertook a radical reduction in course requirements for day students, enabling them to be added to the labour force much sooner. By eliminating exams and much academic material, while condensing technical material, four-year courses were reduced to three years. This was possible, despite the shortening of the school year by two weeks in September (so that students could help with the harvest). To aid in the streamlining of Beal, the matriculation course—the only grade 13 course at the school—was transferred to other, academically oriented schools in the system. Students reduced their extracurricular activities so that they could work on war charities or at after-school jobs; thus, the school shows, open houses, and formal dances were all cancelled, along with some sports activities.

Despite war conditions, Beal saw innovation in other areas. London was the first city in the province to offer sex education, and Beal was the first secondary school in London to receive a dentist's office (as part of a complete health unit, including a full-time nurse). In 1943, Beal became the only secondary school in Ontario to give regular credit for classes in music (*LFP*, November 14, 1945; London Board of Education, 1943, p. 152).

The decade after the war ended was marked by prosperity and the baby boom in Canada. In terms of school life, this was a period of reduced innovative energy, with much of it channelled into future plans dependent on the building of an extension. The school settled into a waiting period of some stability as the students and staff waited for expansion. Teachers tended to be long serving; many in the technical departments were themselves graduates of Beal and had been recruited after several years' experience in industry (K. Leyland, interview; H. Rawson, interview).

Though by 1951 the role of Beal's guidance officer had expanded to the point where a separate department for guidance and placement had to be created, individual differences remained unaddressed: courses for all students remained rigidly structured, with a minimal opportunity to take an optional subject such as music, as well as a few technical subjects for students in the commercial program (AVC, January 8, 1951; May 10, 1951).

With the end of wartime work and the prosperity of the times, extracurricular activities increased again. New traditions appeared, such as an annual graduation dinner (reflecting a better economy), as well as an elected student council (AVC, December 14, 1948; *LFP*, May 24, 1950).

The need for an increased size for the school had become apparent during the war; with the end of that conflict, the AVC, the local board, and the province agreed on an expansion to include a cafeteria, a swimming pool, a library, thirty-three teaching areas, and more than a dozen other rooms and offices. Student accommodation increased from 1,000 to 1,700 in a single stroke. After five years of planning and negotiations, construction started during 1950 but was then stalled by steel restrictions imposed during the Korean War. By September of 1952, the work was sufficiently done to allow the school to close down the staggered timetable after almost 20 years (AVC, November 9, 1944 to March 12, 1953; *LFP*, July 7, 1950; September 1, 1952; December 17, 1953).

The expansion, officially opened in 1953, also benefited the community. After the war, night classes held at Beal had taken a tremendous leap, with enrolment reaching almost 4,500 (*LFP*, December 17, 1953). The swimming pool and cafeteria also were rented out to community groups.

With the freedom granted by the opening of the addition, the period from 1955 to 1968 came to be marked by almost constant innovation and a feeling of euphoria throughout the Beal community. The period in larger scale remained one of prosperity, with the first of the baby boomers starting to move into the high schools. On the commercial side, Beal was one of the first schools to enter the computer age. The department started teaching data processing in the 1959–1960 school year, and the school's own computer—a huge

$100,000 machine—arrived in early 1964 (AVC, December 19, 1953; J. Walsh, interview). At the same time, the commercial division retooled most of its old courses and established several new ones, including a popular clerical practice course focusing on business machines as well as a course in merchandising.

The art program maintained an emphasis on commercial work through the 1950s, but with the 1960s came a real explosion into fine art. With a completely flexible atmosphere and up-to-date techniques taught by talented artists, Beal's art program achieved national prominence, attracting the best art students throughout South Western Ontario.

The period saw two new technical courses aimed at female students, both of them serving as pilots for the provincial department. A two-year cooperative course for nursing assistants first came into operation in 1957, joined eight years later by a course for dietary supervisors. A course in fashion and design was also introduced in 1966.

Other technical areas sponsored a rash of new developments. In 1952, the technical division added a two-year terminal course for those going into an apprenticeship in the building trades. A new course in electronics opened in about 1960 and by 1964 had resulted in an operating television studio, worked for the most part by students outside of class time. In addition, the following technical subjects were either introduced as major options or raised to that status: laboratory technician (1953), auto body repair (1957), plumbing and steam fitting (1963), refrigeration (1963), and industrial chemistry (1964).

In an attempt to tie themselves closely to the needs of the employer, the various technical departments established consultative committees, including industry representatives, from 1962 on.

On the academic side, grade 13 returned to Beal in 1954 with two new five-year courses aimed at university or professional training in business and engineering.

For the first time, a few brave souls broke through the gender barriers that marked the technical areas. In the late 1950s, a course in family living aimed at young men opened; a few years later, individual young women moved into the male technical courses (AVC, December 16, 1953; *LFP*, January 2, 1963; April 26, 1965).

For most of the 1960s, the school hosted a technology course equivalent to a first year at one of the province's technical institutes or colleges of applied technology.

At Beal, two more additions were completed in 1962 and 1965.

The period also saw a revived campaign of attack against Beal through the city's newspaper, with headlines attacking first the teachers for insulting and threatening students and then the students for littering and loitering in the

1950s and rioting in the 1960s (*LFP*, May 28, 1953; December 17, 1953; June 2, 1955; November 20, 1957; June 3, 1967).

In the last twelve years of this study, Beal lost much of its unique character and increased in similarity to the rest of London's secondary schools. In particular, the four years from 1968 to 1972 marked the turning point in the Beal experience, primarily due to a coincidental alignment of trends which were of much longer duration. Yet the school never moved to complete symmetry with the others: External appearances and characteristics continued to mark it out. The province-wide introduction of a subject advancement scheme (the credit system) and stricter rules on teacher recruitment effectively destroyed much of the old structures of learning at Beal. Students no longer travelled in groups from class to class and year to year. Their teachers were no longer artists and artisans (usually Beal graduates) pulled straight into the school. As other employment opportunities created a high turnover in staff, the new nonlocal staff had less interest in a "Beal philosophy" or in placing students directly into jobs (A. Burns, interview; D. Irwin, interview). Many employers agreed with them, with both sides preferring to send students on to the new postsecondary community colleges.

The school plant expanded again in the period with an addition, created mainly to house administrative offices but adding other teaching spaces, completed in 1970.

The late 1960s also saw the flowering of the student revolt. Beal became a haven for hippies (especially in the art program), and recreational drug and alcohol use became a factor in the school environment. At the same time, students became more conscious of their power in the education system and pushed in the classroom or principal's office for modifications to curriculum and pedagogy.

Ernie McTavish, a principal who served only a short term in office, had to reach an accommodation with these students. Under his direction, rules of discipline were relaxed and a more informal school atmosphere promoted, in conjunction with an emphasis on responsibility to accompany the new rights. After McTavish left, a series of principals set out to deal with the repercussions of his actions and as the educational world moved toward the conservative 1980s, tried to reestablish discipline and authority. In this new atmosphere, Beal's millstone reputation reappeared. While student organizers defined "apathy" as the new school problem, the *LFP* (December 15, 1978) returned to old themes and labelled the school "Dope City."

Conclusion

The history of Beal Tech is the story of innovation—with vocational priorities for students and for employers, modified by teacher status concerns.

Every major social change set off curricular repercussions in Beal. The social efficiency movement led to the founding in 1912. Changing vocational definitions led to the commercial integration after 1921. The Depression brought staggered classes and a strong extracurricular program. The Second World War put the school on a total war footing and cut back programs to the bare minimum. Postwar prosperity and the baby boom brought expansion and then a vast range of innovation highlighted by the computer and art programs. The youth revolt brought a change in the structures of school governance.

These changes did not go unopposed. The local paper objected to changes in the 1920s, in the 1950s, and in the 1970s, and was objecting to locational and restructuring changes as late as the 1990s.

CHAPTER SIX

Inside a Research Project

Episodes from a Methodological Diary

C. Anstead

Introduction

There are few books detailing the fascinating life conducted inside a research project. The best existing book on the life inside a research project is *Inside a Curriculum Project* by Shipman, Bolam, and Jenkins (1974). A range of new work reviews the potential of journal keeping for research purposes (Holly, 1989; Malinowski, 1967; Stevens & Cooper, 2009). One of the important methods for developing insights on the life of a school is the methodological diary. The intention of an intensively constructed methodological diary is to note how themes and sources emerge with which to define and delineate the life of a school. The methodological diary is a fairly innovative methodology and grows out of the kind of work that anthropologists and sociologists have developed in conducting their fieldwork.

It is quite easy, when caught up in the detail of the archives and sources for developing the life of a school, to lose sight of emergent themes and theories. The purpose of the methodological diary is to keep a reflective journal of the insights and key questions as they emerge for the researcher.

To model this methodological diary for the reader, we include a six-month selection from the methodological diary that was kept during the research on Beal's school. The diary shows how an ongoing reflexive account keeps close touch with emergent themes and theories and key questions and insights. The methodological diary is, of course, an intensively personal mechanism, and we would expect that each methodological diary would vary considerably in its form and content. Nonetheless, the overall intention is to keep a reflective stream of thought and inquiry going as the everyday details of the school are assembled.

In thinking through the major research engine that drove our inquiry into the life of Beal's school, both writers feel the methodological diary was a crucial part of the matrix of inquiry. By insisting on reflexivity at each point of data collection, the imperative to ask questions and develop insights is sponsored. So I think on reflection we would say the methodological diary was one of the crucial research engines that we developed in looking at the life of a school.

At the beginning, I entered into consideration of primary evidence by reading the report of the Royal Commission on Industrial Training and Technical Education.

I described this source in a brief report, dated January 17, to Ivor Goodson:

> The 1913 Report of the Royal Commission on Industrial Training and Technical Education fills four volumes.... The document consists of three sections, each of which provides information of a different type. Parts I and II present the conclusions and recommendations of the Commission (Part I is an earlier and briefer version of Part II).... Part III discusses the information found in the Commission's travels through England, Scotland, Ireland, Switzerland, Denmark, Germany, France, and the United States.... Part IV summarizes the testimony of witnesses interviewed in Canada. The chapters in this section include descriptions of the extent of vocational schooling already in place in each province, as well as outlining any planned developments. The report also provides examples of the thoughts and suggestions of witnesses who appeared at the hearings; the testimony of employers, employees, educators and other interested parties all can be found. (Anstead, 1994)

As I read through these four volumes, I made notes on information that reflected themes which I had already decided needed investigation and themes which seemed to be emerging from the source. I spent a lot of time looking at the types of schools in other countries because I felt it was important to see the nationality of the model chosen in the case of London. I also made notes on the comments of supporters of this kind of education, especially those representing labour or business groups, and outlined the facilities already existing in this field both in Ontario and in Canada as a whole. As I worked on this source, the issue of the type of nationalism represented by speakers on the question started to interest me. I also spent time recording and analyzing the surrounding rhetoric of the report, which addressed the public justification for vocational studies, revealed the underlying commitment to industrial capitalism held by the members of the Commission, and treated students in a very determinist manner. Unfortunately, I more or less ignored domestic science out of a mistaken assumption that it was not part of what we were doing.

Looking back now (in May of 1991), I can see that all of these interests were external to the "black box" of the school. I focused on issues of institutional and administrative form (for example, day school versus night school or part-time versus full-time) and on the intentions of those behind the movement. In the report, I undertook a bit of speculating on what I referred to as "the ultimate interpretation of the vocational movement." To me at this time, this meant the intentions behind the movement. I did not really look at differences in actual curricula being proposed or used in different places.

Why then did I focus on these external themes? In part, the answer to this lies in the fact that these are, after all, important themes. The issue of intentionality was one raised constantly in the secondary literature I had read. My interest here was reinforced in conversations with Goodson. The question of the national origins of Canadian social institutions and of the forms of Canadian nationalism are ones which have always interested me, and the material I was reading seemed to contradict some of the existing thought in the historical literature. This last point was, however, quite tangential to what was supposed to be the thrust of the project.

Despite these rationalizations, the decision to look at institutions from outside rather than inside reflects a tendency on my part to start out with simple, objective institutional history when commencing the study of an unfamiliar phenomenon. I think I have a sense that the facts of institutional history can be established more easily than the facts of more internal history. This reflects, of course, an attitude towards sources. Sources available for institutional history are more abundant, and generally judged by the history profession as more reliable, than those for more internal, lived experience. Yet in this case, I could have examined information upon internal classroom conditions from the same source that I had confidence in for external institutional history. The reason I did not do so then reflects what was an unsuspected blind spot in my search.

The next primary source that I examined did take me directly into the classroom. This was the file card notes taken by Ian Dowbiggin on the student record cards. I think I was willing to move into the classroom this way because this sort of source was quite familiar to me. I had used similar sources (that is, quantifiable sources listing individual socioeconomic characteristics) in both my M.A. and Ph.D. work. In a report dated January 18, I described the index cards created by Dowbiggin:

> The student record cards from Beal consist of more than three thousand index cards containing a variety of items of information describing the socioeconomic characteristics and careers of individual students. Almost every card contains all of the following items: name, which in most cases serves to indicate gender; age; religion; birthplace; address; parent's occupation; course taken at Beal; last school before Beal; and standing on entry. In addition, some cards contain information on the student's position after leaving Beal, or their reasons for leaving. (Anstead, 1994)

These cards presented a serious methodological problem for me. I had not been part of their collection and, thus, felt unsure about using them without some sort of investigation into the rigour of the collection method.

As I said in the report,

> There are a number of questions which arise after a cursory examination of the student record cards. The first and most important question concerns the origins of these cards. These are not original documents, and thus must be copies of cards or other records at Beal. To be confident in their use, I would want to know more about the original sources, and the rules used for making these copies. A second, and related question concerns the nature of the groups represented by these records. Given the figures for enrolment in the school, the cards for most years seem to be too many to represent just the freshmen, and too few to represent the total enrolment. A third and final problem is the lack of information on post-school careers. Only a small proportion of the cards have any information of this sort, and in many cases this reveals only the name of the employer, but not the type of job. Some additional information might be found in contemporary directories, but as many young people start out their adult lives by leaving the parental home (the one listed on their school records) this will be a difficult task. (Anstead, 1994)

Despite my reservations, I carried out a crude manual analysis of some small groups of cards. In this exercise, I sought to compare the course of study taken by a student with the occupation of the student's parent. Occupations were divided simply into "Manual" or "Nonmanual" at this point in the study.

On reflection, I realize that the file cards were even more imperfect than I then understood. When Dowbiggin collected information from student record cards, he declined to take notes on student performance (marks, subjects studied, attendance, and conduct). From photocopies available to me, I became aware of this omission but at first remained unconcerned. It seemed to me that the socioeconomic data were very useful, while the information missed by Dowbiggin did not seem relevant. It was only later, prodded by a comment from David Labaree, that I saw how important that information was. I now see that the record cards are the only sure way of finding out what subjects were studied in the various years of the various courses. Attendance and conduct marks may be useful in telling us something about student action and could be used as evidence of a counterhegemony. They should be compared to socioeconomic factors.

After dealing with these sources, both of which were ready for me when I joined the project, it was time to start scouting for additional data. On February 20th, I submitted a progress report which described some of the scouting for sources I had carried out. As I detailed in that report:

I have spent some time examining and evaluating a variety of primary sources in several different depositaries. Activities undertaken this month included: a few short discussions with Fred Armstrong on the nature of London's leaders; a review of the photocopied material taken from the Beal archives; and a reading of Fred Israels' *Londoners Remember*, an anecdotal compilation of oral history, which includes a few comments on education in the 1920s. I also spent some time investigating the holdings at the Education Library, at the Regional Room, D. B. Weldon Library, and at the London Room, London Central Public Library. (Anstead, 1994)

After detailing the sources available at Althouse [College], the report continues:

I also spent some time examining the holdings at the Regional Collection, D. B. Weldon Library. This collection does not seem to have anything directly connected with Beal or the technical school. It does, however, have its own collection of *Annual Reports* and *Minutes* of the London Board of Education. These documents are preserved on microfilm, and are more extensive than the ones in the Education library.

Besides these official sources, there are several collections of documents from London teachers, though none of them taught at Beal. I have only examined one of these collections, which turned out to hold several scrapbooks devoted to the history of the London Central Collegiate Institute. During my time at the Regional Room I had a short meeting with Ed Phelps, as a preliminary to a future, more extensive, meeting. (Anstead, 1994)

Next I dealt with the Central Library's London room:

I spent three days at the London Room, London Central Public Library, earlier this month. During this time I ascertained the extent of the library's relevant holdings, spent some time examining a few sources, including the *Tecalogue*... and met with the librarian in charge of the London Room—Glen Curnoe.... Besides the *Tecalogue*, the London Room has some other sources which might prove worth another visit at some future time. The most interesting primary sources are yearbooks and other publications of the local collegiate institutes from various years, but with good coverage of our period.... The London Room also has an extensive collection of local newspapers on microfilm, though most of them are duplicated in the microfilm collection at Weldon. (Anstead, 1994)

The progress report also described some of these sources in more detail; one of them was the *Tecalogue*:

The *Tecalogue* was the name given to the student yearbook at Beal during the period under review. The London Room has six volumes, covering the years 1929–32 and 1934–35. These yearbooks are quite different from those produced today, which are little more than breathless tributes to the graduating class. The *Tecalogue* features articles on a variety of subjects, many of them quite intriguing. Among the more useful articles are: a student essay on why students attend the school, and other passages showing how "Tech" students find themselves different from C.I. students; various articles detailing the types of courses and options available to students; a short history of commercial vocational education in the city, written by a teacher connected with the subject from 1895 to 1935; and a description by H. B. Beal of the staggered system of classes (used to counter overcrowding in the 1930s) which contains a few comments on Beal's personal educational philosophy. I will be preparing a short summary of the information available in this source, similar to the one described below for the Board of Education *Minutes*, but much shorter. (Anstead, 1994)

By the time I prepared this report, I had started to tackle the next major source: the minutes of the Board of Education of the city of London. At that time, I had read most of the volumes from the period 1922 to 1940 inclusive. I had taken notes from these volumes and was in the process of compiling a rather complete summary of the information which I had obtained from this source. In making the notes, and in compiling a summary, I was making very conscious decisions about what to include or exclude. My basic organizing principle was that I should include anything which seemed to be relevant to the emerging themes of the project. Yet it was the study of the minutes (as well as conversations with Goodson and with other colleagues) which was in fact leading to the refinement of older themes and the emergence of new ones, as witnessed by my comments in the report.

I also collected all references to institutional change, to curriculum, and to the status of vocational studies and vocational teachers. I made careful record of such things as members of the board of education and attendance at both the collegiate institutes and the technical school.

Despite this wide range of interest, much information was left unacknowledged. (After all, the point of making notes is to reduce the amount of material that a researcher has to handle.) Many themes of interest to others, such as expenses in connection with specific schools, issues of insurance and safety, or records of attempts to beautify school grounds, were simply ignored, along with hundreds of other bits of information.

The next step in sifting the huge amount of material in the minutes involved creating thematic extracts. Goodson and I had negotiated a narrowing of focus through a series of discussions, which resulted in the emergence of four substantive themes for me to pursue. For each of these themes, I created an extract of the relevant information drawn from the first collection of notes. The extracts focused on social group conflict over technical schooling in London, gender issues, the relationship between the Beal school and employers, and curriculum change in the vocational area at all London secondary schools. As these extracts will now become the primary research tools for the minutes, the information which did not make it into any extract will probably be ignored unless I decide to create a new extract when a new theme emerges. I next considered the annual reports of the board of education. The procedure here was similar to that used on the minutes, though the information available was much scantier. One source of information which I took into account was a

A RESEARCH GUIDE

few lists of diploma winners in various subjects. I used the personal names of the winners as a proxy measure of gender in order to come up with some approximate figures on gender breakdown. The annual reports also allowed me to create a complete, year-by-year, outline of the formal courses of study available at the technical school.

In early May, I undertook an investigation into the information available on the photocopies of student record cards made by Dowbiggin but not available on the file card notes. From these copies, I constructed an outline of subjects included in the various courses of study for the period 1927–1930. As I said in a letter to Goodson dated May 7, "I am confident that this is an accurate model of official curriculum in these courses." This model was constructed through the use of worksheets. I prepared one sheet for each course in each year. The sheet was divided into columns for each year (i.e., first, second, etc.) in the course, and each column was subdivided into gender fields. The rows on the sheet represented the various subjects taught at the school as listed on the course record forms. I then went through the copies and made a note of every subject for which a mark was received by each student and in each of his or her years of study. Altogether I used 120 student/years. In my report to Goodson, I concluded that this evidence supports conclusions in two general areas, those of gender and status concerns. In gender, the evidence showed different patterns in each course for boys or girls. In terms of status concerns, the data showed how various academic subjects were incorporated into the curriculum of the five different courses offered at Beal.

Finally, I have spent time during the past two months on a new draft of our paper on gender. In the course of this work, I have had to make several decisions on the use of evidence and the value of particular pieces of evidence, particularly oral evidence. I plan to report on these decisions in my next section of diary, where my writing can be more current.

Friday, May 24

I am going down to Beal today to meet with Mrs. Glikson, the head of student services and guardian of student records. She will then introduce me to the sources, in particular the student record cards. I thought I should take some time to explain what I expect to do with the student record cards. I am taking with me the set of cards dated "1927" from the Dowbiggin run. The first thing I want to do is find out what these cards represent (i.e. just first year students in 1927, or full student body) and whether they are a sample or a complete data set. I then want to use these cards to create my own data set on the first year cohort from 1927. In other words, the set will include all those entering a first year (not preparatory) course for the first time in September of 1927. I hope that most of the individuals in this cohort are already present on a Dowbiggin card, though some students who entered a preparatory course before taking first year in 1927 may be listed under an earlier year; I will have to search through at least 1925 and 1926 if available. I plan to add certain information to each Dowbiggin card, which was not collected originally. This information will include: the exact class that the student entered in the fall of 1927; information on the student's school career, such as years passed or failed and any transfers to other departments; the marks assigned for conduct and attendance in 1927-8; and the average grade received in the third term of the 1927-8 school year. I hope to do the same thing in future visits for the 1931 and 1935 data sets, though if the work is too unmanageable, I may skip 1931.

At some point I also want to expand the coverage of my subject/course data worksheets which detail the subjects taken by students in each school year of a given course of study. Finally, before leaving Beal, I will take time to find out if any other records exist.

Monday, 3 June

I have now spent several days at the vaults in Beal, and I am more confident in my decisions regarding data collection. I have almost completed the 1927 cards on the basis described in the previous entry. I plan to then move on to the 1931 and 1935 cards; with these cards I will establish the same collections as for 1927, filling in the gaps left by the original Dowbiggin collection. I will add information to the cards on the class attended (which serves to indicate the course of study entered) and on the outcome of the 1927 school year (i.e. pass, fail, quit while failing, quit for job, illness etc.).

Besides the creation of these collections, there are some other things I want to do with these cards. First of all, I want to fill in more worksheets on the subjects taken by students of particular courses of study in particular school and calendar years. (For example, what subjects did male students in 2nd year Matriculation take in 1927?) I am not sure if I will do this for every calendar year, or just for the same years that we have cohorts of cards. Another possibility is to follow the cohorts through, so that we know the subjects of all first year courses in 1927, second year in 1928 and so on. At present the latter possibility seems my likely choice, since it will combine with the card data banks to allow us to talk about the experience of a certain cohort of students.

For each case I will record name, gender, year of entrance, years completed and reasons for leaving the course. I am unsure whether or not to include occupation of parent, but probably will.

The question of the format of this data bank raises some of the issues which I faced in designing the data bank for the more general collections of data. I decided in the first place to have Karen (the project secretary of the Ruccus Research Unit) set up a data base which would include the 1927 general first year cohort, and the 1927 special commercial class. These two groups can easily be separated for analytical purposes by the statistical software. I asked her to set up a matrix which included the following information for each student: case number, gender, class entered, address code, birthplace, parent's occupation, standing at entrance, 1927 outcome, career at school, date leaving school, placement occupation, and marks for attendance, conduct and academic average. Karen will enter some of this information directly, while I will enter the information which calls for some interpretation of the remarks on the card. I have decided to use case numbers instead of names for ethical reasons; it should make it easier for us to allow other researchers access to the data base at some future time. We can still retrieve names if we need them from the hard copy cards, which have both case number and name included. The address code is at present being left blank. I hope in future to divide the city into regions (perhaps based on wards, perhaps on a 1970s division of the city by municipal agents into functional sections—which will be more useful as we move towards the present—or perhaps on the basis of traditional divisions such as East London, South London, etc.). At present the occupational categories (parental and placement) are being entered simply as job titles, but at some future date it will be necessary to recode them as proxies for social class. Before this though, I think I will have some long conversations with Ivor Goodson on the issue.

Speaking of long conversations, I spent several hours last week discussing oral history with Jan Trimble and Prof. J. Hyatt at the history department. Professor Hyatt teaches the graduate oral history course in the department (only two exist in the country they tell me). Jan Trimble is involved with the course, and has extensive experience in the practice of oral history. During these discussions, they provided me with advice on methodology, outlined some of their own experiences, and suggested sources for further reading. I also raised several issues which I felt lay at the theoretical heart of the use of oral history. They answered my questions about the role of the interviewer by making a parallel with the generation of any historical document. Most of the concerns which I brought up were answered by saying that a well-trained practitioner would avoid any obvious contamination of the evidence, though absolutely value-free interviewing was impossible. In fact, at the core of their defence of oral history was the argument that all the concerns I raised about verification, the role of the interviewer/historian, and the ethical use of data, could equally be raised about more traditional sources. Professor Hyatt argued that the use of oral history should make any historian less of a "document determinist" and more concerned about the verification and use of his or her documentary sources.

Monday, June 10

I have now spent three weeks in the vault at Beal. I have managed to complete my updating of the 1927 and 1931 cards originally collected by Dowbiggin. I will not be able to update the 1935 cards, because the originals have been sent away for microfiche recording. At some future time we can probably gain access to these, but that will require a whole new set of negotiations. For the 1931 cards, I divided them into the same sets as for 1927; I did not, however, include quite as much information. The only thing I added to Dowbiggin's notes was to record the outcome of the 1931 school year for each student. I think that less than half of all first year students successfully finished the year. I did not record age on these cards, but at the suggestion of Ivor Goodson I will go back and do this for those who quit school, to see if they were leaving illegally. One other item which neither Dowbiggin nor myself collected was the religious affiliation of the students. I am concerned that this might represent a weakness in our data collection, but to return for this information for the 1927 and 1931 cohorts would represent a lot of working hours. As a temporary measure, Goodson and I have decided that I will collect religious data for the matriculation students when I set up that separate data bank. If an analysis then seems to show religion playing a role in student course selection or outcomes, I will have to go back for 1927 and 1931 information.

Some of the original 1931 cards which Dowbiggin made notes from have gone missing. Since most of them represented students who were still in school in 1935, I think they are also in the microfiche bundle. Roughly fifty such cards are missing, representing a potentially serious gap in our records. I have thus decided to use some of the Dowbiggin cards in my 1931 cohort data bank, though I will note in the comments field that these cards were "not found." I decided whether or not to use a given "not found" card in the following way. Any special commercial cards were accepted, since this was a one-year program in most cases, and no one went directly to fourth year in this department. For the other cards, anyone with previous high school experience was considered a probable transferee to second year or higher, and left out of the data bank. The remaining commercial cards were all used. The technical cards, however, were further divided. Those students with High School Entrance standing were added to the data bank; those with only grade seven or eight standing were probably prep course students and not added.

A consideration of the cards still in the vault raises a few problems with this procedure. For instance, some H.S.E. [high school entrance] standing tech. students went directly into a special tech. course. In a few cases, students who took a year of prep and then went into commercial studies had a new card filled in for their second year. If this happened, a student who entered the general commercial course in 1932 after a year of prep, would be collected under Dowbiggin's procedures as a 1931 entrant in the commercial department. My procedure would then put such a student in the first year comm. course in 1931. Both of these problems are statistically rare, and can probably be safely ignored, though the addition of the "not found" comment does allow these cases to be dropped from the data base or ignored in calculations if further reflection demands this. At present I feel that it would be more harmful to ignore these "not found" cards altogether.

June 12

During my time in the vault I have made a new discovery, the presence of record cards from the very beginning of the school up to 1926. From a reference in one of Dowbiggin's memos it is apparent that he was aware of these cards but chose to ignore them, probably because they have much less information than the later cards. These cards simply list name, gender, address, parent's name and course. I plan to use these cards to create new cohorts of students. I will supplement them by reference to contemporary directories, which will be a rather long job. The logical thing to do seems to be to extend the existing four-year spacing of cohorts backwards. Thus new cohorts will be created for 1915, 1919, and 1923. Because the school started in 1912, I also wanted to create a cohort for this year, though it would lead to an ugly three-year gap. In conversation with Goodson, though, it was decided to do a cohort for each year from 1912 to 1915. These were years of very small attendance so such a path would not involve a lot more work, and should provide a greater breadth of information. It also has the opportunistic advantage of eliminating the three-year gap and making the spacing of cohorts over four-year periods seem a logical decision in the face of a complete run of cards. Because these early cards have little information on the exact level of study a student entered, the cohorts will be based simply on year of first entrance to the school. Thus only the cohorts for 1927 and 1931 will be refined to mark the exact year of entrance to the first year of a general course. Those before and after will have to remain unrefined.

June 24

I have now finished a second run at the 1931 cards. Since I was going back to get age at quitting, I decided to also record the religion of the students from their cards.

Most cards give a specific denomination, but some say only "Protestant." Some of the denominations listed will need further investigation. For instance, many cards list the "English Church" under religion, which seems to mean something other than "Church of England." I suspect it is the name of a specific congregation, probably an Anglican one. I have also encountered several cards with "Gospel Hall" on them, which I will have to investigate. Finally, I have recorded cards which say "synagogue" or "Hebrew" as Jewish.

Another task which I pursued during the last week was the creation of a data base of matriculation students. I divided matriculation students into two groups, those who entered first year, and those who transferred into the program at a later point. I recorded the name, the years successfully completed, reason for leaving, year of entrance and gender for all matriculation students. In addition, I recorded the standing of transferee students, and the year of the program they entered. Again I chose to give these students case numbers for future use. Students entering first year received a case number with the prefix "M," while transferees received a number starting in "T." Altogether I collected information on 435 matriculation students. This new data collection is incompatible with the other ones in that it is not a calendar-based cohort, and it includes students in years other than first. In addition, there will be overlap between the year of entry cohorts and the matriculation database, since some matriculation students started their course in one of the years collected.

June 27

I have now finished with all the student record cards. I collected information on those students who entered the school, (at whatever level) in one of these years: 1912, 1913, 1914, 1915, 1919, or 1923. The number of cards collected for each of these years is approximately: 10 for 1912, 50 for 1913, 90 for 1914, 110 for 1915, 80 for 1919 and 300 for 1923. Although I had originally wanted to use each of these for a cohort, I am thinking of making some changes. A comparison with the total attendance at the school makes the number of cards collected for 1912 seem too low. Possibly the cards from this year represent only those students who stayed in the school for two or more years. In other words, maybe in the first year, cards for students who left were discarded. The 1913, 1914 and 1915 cards seem to be an adequate representation of entering students, and represent over three-quarters of the full-time student body. The 1919 and 1923 cards represent about a half of the student body; this probably results from students staying longer rather than from a problem with the records. There is another possibility as far as 1919 cards are concerned; the fact that the school used bound registers in the late 'teens may have affected the use of cards. Very few 1918 cards exist in the file, but registers for 1918 can be found. I have no direct evidence that such registers were used in 1919; if they were, the existing 1919 cards may represent students who stayed in the system and thus needed cards when the school returned to their use.

The questions now under consideration are whether or not to use the earliest cards, and whether or not to refine the cohorts by eliminating special or senior transferee students. My thinking here is to ignore the cards for 1912, while combining the cards from 1913, 1914 and 1915 to create a single cohort. As to the second question, it would seem logical to eliminate such students so that the cohort would be consistent with others. There is one problem though; some new incoming male students apparently went directly to the class that other male students took in second year. This bears some explaining. In the period up to 1923 at least, the classes were designated by letters. As a student went through the school, he or she would move up from "D" to "A." It seems that all girls had to start at "D," but some boys were able to start at "C." From what I've noticed as I collected this information, all boys with HSE standing, and some others, did this. (One note on a student record card written much later equates the "D" class with grade 8, though I think this is too simple.) I will eliminate all those who started at the school in the "B" or "A" classes, and keep all the "D" and "C" students in the cohort. (When I speak of "eliminating" some cards, I mean in terms of putting them into the computer data files; the hard-copy record cards will not be destroyed but will be saved though not used.)

While working on these cards, I have been thinking about the issue of residence. One simple solution to determining student residence is simply to code the elementary school as a proxy for residence. For those students who transferred from a C.I., we will have to look up their address to determine into which elementary school district it falls. At present though, residence is not a priority, as I have no plans to use it.

Finally, since I have finished all the cards in the vault, I have had to turn to other sources. One such source is the student registers mentioned above. Specifically, I have found two registers which record the attendance of all male students in 1918-1919 except for those in the "D" class. These registers contain things other than attendance, including address, parent or guardian, parent's occupation, and religion. Thus there is wonderful material for analysis, but material which is incompatible with the major cohorts I have been creating. Yet as a snapshot of the more senior grades, I cannot ignore it. I am planning to photocopy both registers, and decide how to use the data later.

The registers exhaust the student records in the vault; however, simply in looking around as I work, I have seen a variety of boxes, volumes and other records which seem to date from the period of our study. I asked Mrs. Glikson for permission to go into these sources, feeling that this would not be a controversial question given that I already had access to student records. She, however, was unwilling to deal with anything outside of her direct responsibility (i.e. student records). She suggested I speak with someone in administration. I did so, and have been referred back to Mr. Parker, the principal, who was unavailable. I will call him next week, and feel certain that I can get his approval for this examination. He has already indicated his support for the project, but I did not want to be in the position of rooting through a locked vault without someone's specific permission to do so.

July 18

I have been successful in obtaining permission to extend my surveys in the vault, and have spent one day doing so. I examined every book, box, drawer and shelf in the vault to find material relevant to the case study. After collecting all this material, I have started the process of note-taking. The first source examined in detail was a volume entitled *Results of Departmental Examinations*. This book contains forms filled out at the school, concerning pupils who were to take the provincial examinations for middle and upper schools. They cover the period of the 1930s and 1940s. Each annual report lists the pupils by name, and indicates in which subject(s) he or she will sit exams. I made notes on the reports for 1931, 1935, and 1940. My concern in this instance was not with names, but numbers; I wanted to know how many students wrote these exams, since this again would reveal the effectiveness of the matriculation program. According to these documents, 18 students wrote examinations in 1931, 30 in 1935 and 31 in 1940.

The second volume I examined contained pay sheets for the school staff during the period of our study. These listed annual or semi-annual salaries for each teacher, but did not mention teachers' Subjects or departments. I hope to link the names of teachers which I found in this source to their Subject. This will then allow me to see if the particular subject taught affected the wage received. I have to admit, though, that I think the answer here will be a negative one. Again, I copied out the lists only for selected years spread over the study period.

After dealing with these sources, I turned to the collection of the *Minutes* of Advisory Vocational Committee. The vault contains a complete run of these records for the period of our study; reading them will be the work of a week or more. They are much fuller than the summaries and reports recorded in the Board of Education *Minutes*. The early years consist almost entirely of reports made by Beal, with a few notations of Committee motions and votes in response to Beal's suggestions. These provide a very extensive look at Beal's ideas and philosophies regarding his school. As with earlier sources of this sort, I am taking notes on all things which seem relevant to our current or future concerns.

July 23

The work I have been doing in the last few days provides an interesting example of the implication of research and writing. Though this diary has only revealed information on the steps I have taken in researching this topic, at the same time I have been involved in writing. At one level, I have been working on outlines and ideas for papers to come later. At a second level, I have been working on a paper on commercial education, based on an early draft by I. Dowbiggin and I. Goodson. This working paper has changed focus considerably over the last few months; in the latest round of talks with Goodson, we decided to make the focus of the paper the curriculum changes that took place in commercial education at the Technical school, and their relation to professional status.

August 9

After spending several more days at Beal, I have gone a fair ways into the AVC *Minutes*. Yesterday, however, I decided to depart from my research calendar for external reasons.

To be specific, I had to go to the main campus to locate some secondary sources, and felt I might as well make a day of it. I took with me the index cards for the 1913, 1914 and 1915 student cohorts. The information on these cards, transferred manually from the student record cards in the vault, has already been entered into the database by Karen Keohen. These early cards (and those for 1919 and 1923) contain no information on parental occupation, but do include parental names and addresses. My intention is to use local directories to determine parental occupation from the information on student cards. I started that process yesterday, and immediately encountered the historiographic problem of linkage. In other words, when can we be reasonably certain that the parent of a student and a person mentioned in a directory are the same individual?

August 17

Ivor and I spent the morning discussing various aspects of the project, chief among them the issue of class. I am at the point where I want to start analysis of the data, but to do so requires some aggregation of occupational titles into categories, presumably based on some theory of social class. We decided to define occupational categories which will be useful in the long run, and which we do not see as necessarily proxies for class. At present we see London's class system consisting of three groups: a tiny elite, a middle class and a working class. None of these groups are defined by occupation alone, though occupation serves as a constraint. (The theory behind this reasoning will be detailed in our research publications.) We decided to create seven working categories for the organisation of occupational titles. These categories are: professionals; teachers; other non-manual; skilled manual; unskilled manual; farmers; and not classified. This is a flexible system, since these categories can be aggregated easily. The correspondence with class goes as follows. The elite consists of the wealthiest families, and may be drawn from any of the first four categories (since a factory owner may still refer to himself by a craft title). The middle class includes all other non-manual workers, and some skilled manual workers. The working class consists of the remainder of skilled manual workers, and all the unskilled. Farmers and others do not correspond to a specific class.

September 18

Altogether, I have spent close to a month concentrating on writing and reading the secondary literature. The only "undirected" primary research I have completed in this period has been linking names from the student cards for the years 1913, 1914, and 1915, to local directories. In the end, I consulted directories for the period 1913 to 1916. I would estimate that I found an occupation for the parent or household head for at least eighty per cent of the cards. (This estimate can be checked after either Karen or I enter the new information on the cards.) Of the remainder, about one half could not be linked because of inadequate address information on the student cards. This included those cards without any address, and those with just an area post office address. Because the directories also listed outlying towns in the county, I was able to link some students (less than one per cent of the total) from these places, which I had not expected.

I have received permission from Ms. Pat Daly, the office manager at Beal S.S. [Secondary School], to go into the 75th anniversary collection. According to Daly, this is housed rather haphazardly in a small room at the school. I hope to start work there next Tuesday. I am also looking

A RESEARCH GUIDE   69

to start the oral interview process soon. I would like to publish the letter calling for subjects within the next three weeks.

October 2

I have now spent two and a half days in the 75th anniversary archives at Beal Secondary School. They are in room *C212* at the school, which is primarily used as the working site of a massive photocopier. Thus I have been mistaken several times for a photocopier repair person. The archives are stored rather haphazardly and without any thought to proper preservation techniques. They seem little used. They do, however, contain a wealth of information, and some real research gems. The pieces of evidence which most impressed me were: a photographic collection including at least one hundred images from the period under review; a school notebook; a scrapbook started by Beal; and an official announcement from the mid 1920s. A number of other documents are included in the collection, including several scrapbooks.

After an initial sorting and listing of the contents of these archives, I turned to the photograph collection. Most of these pictures are not identified. Some of them have been identified by unknown parties, and some of the resulting identifications are clearly incorrect. I was able to determine the approximate or exact date for the majority of the photos. Several clearly came from the period before the new building was built. They show cramped basement rooms. The rest show the much roomier facilities in the new building, thus presenting a clear image of status change. Some of the pictures from the new building were featured in a newspaper article of 1918, and clearly can be no later than this. Since one of the photos includes the exact date (November, 1918) on the blackboard, it seems that this group of pictures was probably shot specifically for the story. Some of the other photos are featured in clippings found in the scrapbooks, allowing for effective dating. Finally, the rest can be assigned a rough date by examining the students' dress and classroom facilities.

I concentrated on the classroom shots in my study of the pictures, and ignored posed group shots or scenes from school plays. Besides evidence of very different physical accommodations, the pictures revealed a clear gender division in all classes, and hinted at pedagogical practice in the way that almost every teacher was pictured on the boundaries of the class, standing with arms folded. Individual photos revealed other information which I noted.

I brought the notebook and announcement to Althouse for photocopying and then returned them. The notebook offers a unique glimpse of classroom life. It covers a domestic science class for first year commercial students. The general rules copied by the student say a lot about gender assumptions. The school announcement goes into great detail about the content and purpose of each course at the school. I have not yet made a detailed examination of either of these sources, since I can do that at my leisure. My first look at the notebook, however, has made me consider adding a request for such memorabilia to our letter soliciting oral testimony.

Today I started into the scrapbooks. I am leaving the book started by Beal for last, since it seems most interesting. It apparently includes quotes on the philosophy of education and other matters that impressed Beal. Thus it will tell us something more about the man who was so influential in the establishment and operation of the school. The scrapbooks I read today were titled "Advertisements and Readers." At first I did not know what "Readers" were, but after some time it became clear that they are what we call "Press Releases." Thus the scrapbooks contain a copy of every advertisement ordered by the school, and all press releases printed. Often the same release was printed in identical form by two or three local newspapers. The advertisements support my reading of the annual reports of the Board of Education as far as changes in courses are concerned. The press releases include statements of general philosophy which have some interest, and sometimes include other items of interest. Among such items is an acknowledgement that the girls' technical course, while based on home-making, does prepare young women for jobs in certain "feminine" industries. This is one of several half-hidden references I have found to this orientation; I think it will be an important theme when we write about domestic science.

While I was working at the school this morning, I met Mr. Bob Gladwell, who introduced himself as the manager of these archives. At first he seemed a little resentful that he had not been informed of our project, or of my presence in his collection. After we talked for a while, this attitude seemed to fade. At the end of our discussion, I asked him if he could tell me anything about the people who lent material for the 75th anniversary. Mr. Gladwell replied that he had typed up a list of lenders and their possessions. He was not sure where the list had gone, but thought it might be somewhere in the archives. I will therefore have to take another look through the collection. I gave him a business card in case he remembers where the list is, or has anything else to discuss.

October 21

I have now finished my examination of the Beal 75th anniversary archives. I never did find the list of donors, but I did turn up a number of school "announcements" from the period under review. These pamphlets average about 20 pages each, and are dedicated to describing the various courses at the school in some detail. I have made complete photocopies of a selection of these pamphlets covering as much chronological ground as possible. The scrapbook started by Beal proved to be a true goldmine. The clippings Beal underlined, and quotations he copied, give some more indication of his personal ideology. In addition, the scrapbook contains a variety of official school reports on things like enrolment (including gender divisions for a period much earlier than otherwise available), placements, individual withdrawals with reasons given, and staff. Again I have made copies of a number of these reports. Therefore, though I have finished with the sources physically located at Beal, I still have a lot of photocopied material to consider.

It is now time to determine the next step in my research strategy. Among the tasks to undertake are: examination of holdings at the Board of Education, at the Archives of Ontario, and at the Public Archives of Canada; statistical manipulation of the student card data bank; and initiation of the oral testimony collection.

While on the topic of oral testimony, I should mention a discussion that I had with one of the teachers at Beal, who had been a student in the 1950s. During the conversation, I mentioned the oral interviews that had already been carried out for the project. This teacher was quite outspoken in his opinion that one of our informants (a name was mentioned, but I'm not sure it belongs here) was not a "typical" teacher. He said that this teacher was in fact heartily disliked by both staff and students, due to certain autocratic tendencies. This raises some issues about the associated oral testimony. Is there such a thing as a "typical" teacher, and should we seek them out? Should evidence of behaviour deemed inappropriate in the post-war era influence our reading of the oral testimony from an earlier period? Is it possible that a teacher placed in such a defensive position at the end of a long career might present his or her testimony as a self-serving illustration of his or her ultimate good sense? These are just concrete examples of the sort of dilemmas we will face when we move into the oral testimony stage of the project.

November 12

Ivor and I met last week to discuss the working agenda of this project. I sent Ivor a long memo asking him about the projected timing for various papers, especially the papers dealing with the Commercial Department, the Matriculation Course. In the course of our discussion, we decided to try a new approach to our collaboration. In the case of the commercial paper, I basically wrote the piece with suggestions from Ivor. Though this might seem very one-sided for a paper published under two names, other factors served to balance the books: I did make use of Ivor's store of expertise, I was working for Ivor, and I expected to receive benefits in other areas, such as space in books under contract. For the matriculation paper, though, we decided to try a more direct collaboration. I have completed collecting the evidence which I wanted to use in the matriculation paper. This collection is based on the fact that I originally noticed some discontinuity between the rhetoric and reality of social efficiency and a matriculation program. (It might thus appear that I proceeded in the manner suggested by Foucault, by looking for reversals and changes in a discourse; in fact I am now breaking Foucault's rules by searching for the origins of this discontinuity.) While I already had some ideas about how the evidence I had assembled was related, I was still searching for a good theoretical handle on the paper. I had intended to produce this theoretical understanding and incorporate it into the paper before handing it over to Ivor. Instead, Ivor has taken the existing paper—little more than a calendar of facts assembled to an implicit scheme of interpretation—and will produce the first real draft. We will see how this method of proceeding works.

While Ivor is working on this, I will be concentrating on finishing the data collection and interpretation for the student cards. This involves determining parental occupations for the 1919 and 1923 cohorts from directories, entering this new information into DataPerfect, transforming the DataPerfect files into SPSS files, and producing SPSS jobs which will affect the desired statistical manipulation.

November 22

During the last two weeks I have completed the collection of data for the 1919 and 1923 cohorts, following the algorithms already discussed. I will start entering this data next week.

November 28

I am presenting my seminar on the matriculation paper tomorrow. To make a reasonable presentation, I have had to come up with my own theoretical interpretation of the data I have collected, even though Ivor is working on the argument for the actual paper. I thought it might be useful to record my interpretation here, for later comparison with the finished paper.

After starting with a brief description of the overall project, I will explain that I see the matriculation option as a window for exploring some of the disjunctions between rhetoric and reality in the history of the technical school. In his first few years as principal at the school, H.B. Beal followed social efficiency programs with a vengeance. He visualized his school's functions purely in terms of preparing students for future roles determined by the needs of London's society and economy. He looked to those involved in the local economy for guidance in terms of subjects and content taught. He ignored the existing framework of ritual categories such as grades, classes or subjects.

In 1918, however, all this changed. The school changed from a general industrial school into a technical high school. The whole framework of courses, grades and classes was implemented. The introduction of the matriculation course, in particular, represented an abandonment of one primary aspect of Beal's version of social efficiency: his school was no longer a completely terminal institution. At this point I will use the argument of John Meyer to explain what happened. Simply put, Beal was not powerful enough to challenge the existence of institutionalized educational definitions.

Yet this was not a complete defeat for Beal. While acknowledging the necessity of accepting official and pervasive definitions of legitimate education, Beal continued to think of his school primarily in terms of its social efficiency. He continued to encourage lay participation in curriculum-making. In addition, an examination of the reality of the matriculation program shows that few students took it. (Only 7 to 10 per cent of incoming first year students signed up for the course.) Few of those students completed it. (Only one-fifth of matriculation students completed at least four years in the course.) In other words, Beal found the course necessary for reasons of status, but did not support it warmly. I will conclude the presentation with a short postscript regarding its effects on student experience. I see it as another small step in the process by which the student body was increasingly segregated and stratified in this period.

I will be passing out a sheet with two tables on it at the seminar. These are updated versions of tables in the draft which I gave Ivor. I have to update them because the originals were flawed. Table 1 in the draft, concerning choice of incoming students, had incorrect figures for 1927. This resulted from the fact that Karen ran stats on this cohort before it was completely finished. Unfortunately, I assumed that the report she gave me represented the whole cohort, and used it in the paper. On preparing for my seminar, I discovered my mistake, and made a new run on the whole cohort.

Table 2, which discusses student outcome in the matriculation course, had to be changed too. Originally, the table claimed to track all students who entered between 1927 and 1934. However, when reviewing the data, I noticed that almost all students who completed the full five years of the course came from the group entering in 1927 or 1928. I think that the data set used for the first version of the table is incomplete. Some cards for students still in the system after 1934 have apparently been moved to the card files for after 1934, while others remain in the 1927-34 files. By restricting my table to students entering in 1927 or 1928 though, I can be confident that this problem does not exist. Incidentally, this problem only affects the special data collected for the matriculation students. Although some of the student cards for the general 1931 cohort must have been missing when I made my survey supplementing Dowbiggin's original collection, they would have been present when Dowbiggin did his work, since the cards for 1935 and beyond were then present in the vault.

December 19

I had a meeting with Ivor this week to discuss progress on the project. We decided that my work would proceed in four areas. First, I would finish up the SPSS runs which I have started. After entering the parental occupations for the earliest cohorts into DataPerfect, I am now spending most of my time checking the data, and creating SPSS job files to read and recode the data. Because of the technical nature of these tasks, I have created a second Case File, which contains print outs of all the steps I have taken (or will take) to code and analyze the data. This will explain the process to any other researcher who is interested at a later date.

My second priority (we decided) is to write a letter to the editor of the *London Free Press*, which will ask for volunteer oral witnesses. In the letter, I will also ask for anyone possessing school notebooks or relevant private journals or papers to contact us.

My third priority is a more typical research assistant job. Ivor has a list of sources which he wants to consult in his reworking of the constituency paper. These sources include copies of the 1914 regulations, as well as anything relevant to the period from 1912 to 1919. I am to gather these together and provide them to him.

When I have done that, I will present the results of the SPSS analysis in the form of a long report containing lots of tables. This will serve as the primary source of data for our writing of future articles, though the generation of new tables will always be possible.

January 13

Within the last week, I have sent off two letters which should be important in our work. One is the letter to the editor of the *London Free Press*, and the other is the letter to the special collections librarian at Teachers College, Columbia.

January 21

Last week I completed my collection of sources for Ivor, and forwarded it to him. I am now working on the ROP III paper (Ruccus Occasional Papers—an internal research publication at the University of Western Ontario), which is helping my thinking on the whole project, since I am trying to use it to deal with the central issue in the whole thing. I am also working on my data report; at present Karen is working up the first few tables into a presentable form. The letter to the editor has not yet been published. I phoned the *Free Press* and was told that it will probably be published, but as it is not topical, they can make no promise about when it will appear.

I have decided that it is time I went to the Ontario Archives. Both Ivor and I feel that the events preceding the conversion of the London Industrial School into a technical high school are very important for our understanding of the school's history. We expect that there will be correspondence on this issue in the files of the technical education department of the Ministry of Education. Finding them will be my primary research aim when I travel to Toronto.

February 3

Both of the letters have now produced results. The response from Columbia U. was both heartening and depressing. The staff at the archives there are quite willing to help. However, they can do nothing until we determine what course Beal took. To do this involves opening his academic records.

The letter referred me to an official in the registrar's office. When I contacted that person, I was told that only Beal's estate or heirs could make this request.

After hearing this, I phoned a lawyer (my sister actually) and was told that her firm could trace Beal's estate and heirs, and get us a copy of his will, for less than one hundred dollars. Ivor gave me the green light to make this arrangement.

February 6

On Tuesday of this week I travelled to the Archives of Ontario in Toronto. It was a disappointing visit. I made contact with the Archivist specifically responsible for the Department of Education. Between us, we determined that the material I need is not at the archives. Apparently, the department weeded through its records before transferring them in the early 1950s. Officials eliminated anything thought to be of no historic value. This included all departmental files on specific vocational schools. Thus there is an empty file folder titled "London Technical and Commercial High School." A search of various finding aids and indices for other departmental files turned up nothing which seemed relevant. I did find one promising source in the private papers collection: the papers of Canon Cody, the Minister of Education for a brief period at the end of World War One. When I examined his papers, though, I could find nothing specifically referring to London, and little dealing with educational matters at all.

It seems likely that the correspondence I was seeking no longer exists. The project has thus found itself hindered by the intractable selection of the past, a selection presumably influenced by the dominant view of history as "Acts and Facts" in the 1950s.

February 13

I have now set up the interviews for next week. I will spend four days on the road, with two appointments per day. I could probably slot in three per day, but I do not wish to rush anyone, leave a fruitful interview before the speaker is done, or arrive late. I will spend the first two days with former technical students (all male). I will spend the following two days with women who attended commercial courses. I have asked Karen to accompany me on these two days. I think that her presence might put female subjects at ease, and thus encourage greater participation in the interview process. In fact, I have asked Karen to take a dominant role on the last day of taping, while I act as her assistant. Again, I am not sure if this will change anything, but I want to try. Finally, Karen's presence will protect me from any unforeseen complication arising from my being alone in a woman's home. I simply do not want to be put in that position.

February 24

I spent last week interviewing former students at the school. In general, it was an enjoyable experience, and provided material of immense value to the project. At the same time, I feel that I could have collected even more material. In particular, I think that I should have asked more questions about their perceptions of the context of the time. I tended to ask only about schooling, not about their broader experience of the times.

My first interview was with Mr. H. Kennedy. I tried to allow all the subjects to set the procedural rules for the interview; Mr. Kennedy wanted a question and answer format. His answers were informative and to the point. Though the interview was short, it contained a lot of information. If we transcribe any interviews, this is one I would suggest.

I also interviewed Mr. N. Hopkins on my first day. This was the longest interview I conducted, and took much of the afternoon. Mr. Hopkins had been a student at Tech. in the 1920s, and later became a teacher. He opened the interview with a long discussion of the school based on some notes he made in advance. In particular, he dealt with the sort of projects technical students undertook at the time. At times his thoughts turned to his years as a teacher. His wife, Edna, had also been a student and teacher at Tech., in the field of domestic science. At times she joined the discussion, adding valuable commentary. I might seek to interview her by herself at a future time. When I brought out the consent form, Mr. Hopkins was reluctant to sign. I left the form with him, and returned on Thursday. At that point I realized that his hesitancy sprang from his memories of teaching days. He felt that some of the lighter anecdotes might cast some disrespect on the principal at the time. Thus we added a condition to the consent form, granting his permission for use of the material which covered the period up to 1940, but not later.

On Tuesday morning, I called on Mr. A. Buchwald. Mr. Buchwald had prepared three pages of notes, which he asked me to read, and then question him. Mr. Buchwald was very hesitant about the use of the tape recorder, so I did not tape the session. I made as full a report of the interview as I could immediately afterwards, but I think that the lack of a tape limits the value of this contact. That afternoon I visited Mr. G. Walsh. He proved to be an excellent subject, and one whom I would gladly approach if a second round of interviews was needed.

On Wednesday, Karen and I started to call on former commercial students. The first person we interviewed was Mrs. E. Richardson. Unfortunately, I neglected to check the recording level on our machine. It had been jarred out of position, so the resulting recording is very quiet, though still useable.

That afternoon, Karen and I met with Mrs. K. Mrs. K. does not want her name used in our reports, so we will have to go with the initials "M.K." Mrs. K. was still a good subject. She also presented us with several shorthand and bookkeeping texts, which she remembered using in her special commercial course. The bookkeeping text has a lot of writing in the margins, seeming to indicate which sections were used in class. Mrs. K. confirmed that she was the only one to use that particular text, and most of the others.

On Thursday, we met with Mrs. M. Allison. Mrs. Allison provided a very interesting interview. She has clear memories of class-based attitudes and of barriers between the special commercial class and the other students. This is another interview which I would consider transcribing completely.

Our last interview was with Mrs. E. Smith. Mrs. Smith preferred the question and answer format. She identified herself in one of the pictures from the Beal 75th anniversary book, making an interesting link to another sort of document.

March 23

I have spent most of the last month writing papers, but last week was another oral history week. I interviewed another seven former students (some with the help of Karen Keohen) I am starting to realize what these interviews are contributing to my understanding of Beal history. For the most part, it seems an incremental process. Though no single interview would give me confidence in my mental reconstruction of the past, the mosaic of new detail and repeated patterns I am finding is allowing me that confidence. In other words, I feel I have a fairly accurate picture of classroom life in the school between the wars. I have images of the teaching styles of many different teachers. I can visualize the sort of projects technical students undertook. I can imagine what the atmosphere in class, or in the halls, was like. But to reach this level of confidence, it was necessary to undertake the fifteen interviews that I have conducted. No subject recalled with sweeping clarity all these things; I probably would not have trusted anyone who did, at least until I verified it.

Of course some interviews have been more fruitful than others. I tend to divide the interviews into three types. First are those which did not go well. Some former students cannot stay on topic in their reminiscences. Despite a number of attempts by myself, or Karen, they will talk about the present, or totally unconnected past experiences. I have to admit here that my style of interviewing is to go with the subject's flow, and so I probably do not do enough to force the issue. Even these interviews can produce useful information—it just takes more work to find it. Of the seven interviews done last week, two fell into this category. Yet each did have at least one or two pieces of information which adds immeasurably to the whole picture.

The second type of interview is the norm. In these interviews, the subject stays on topic, answers questions in useful ways, and provides a lot of information to add to our brick by brick reconstruction of "Tech." In this sort of interview, the schooling experience is invariably presented in rosy tones. Frequently comparison to the present system of education is made, with many negative comments about the latter. The main themes of this sort of interpretation are: students were disciplined and showed respect for their teachers; every teacher—without exception—was good, and many went beyond the call of duty; and all students, whatever their socioeconomic background, were treated the same. The positive view of their school days probably results partly from the selection process; those people who most enjoyed or valued their school experience were most likely to answer our ad. Yet, I would not want to dismiss the positive out of hand; there is probably some truth behind the platitudes.

Finally, the third type of interview is rare. A few former students present more critical or analytical views of their past. Two such interviews took place last week. These students still have a generally positive view of "Tech.," and present their school days as the "best of times." Yet they are also willing to say that certain teachers were not very good (or even unbalanced in one case). They can point to some types of discrimination, either in the school, or on the part of outsiders describing the school. There are still large gaps in our understanding of the school. None of the students were aware of any tensions or conflict at the staff level. They tend to think of the principal purely in terms of his responsibility for discipline. So, while the interviews are tremendously helpful in dealing with some of our questions, they leave others completely unanswered.

April 16

I have been spending the last two weeks doing all the data runs on the student record cards. The timing of this relates to a practical problem: the computer with SPSS and the data files on it will be taken out of my office at the end of this month. I have been coding new variables from existing information, particularly on placement. The grouping of occupational titles into broad categories for the placement positions poses some problems. Certain jobs which are just jobs for adolescents seem to say little about student life chances. In other words, I'm not sure that the first job many students take on leaving high school has any effect on their career. I am thinking of those who become "messengers," "errand boys," "copy boys," "stock boys," "paper boys," or "pin boys." At present I have set up the codes so that students going to these positions are not classified, while students who go to adult positions are.

April 22

For an experiment, I ran some multiple regression analysis on one of my data cohorts. Setting up the regression equation itself is quite a task. I did not realize how complex it is. Anyways, I found out that all variables involved in multiple regression have to be coded as numeric figures. Thus I have had to go back and recode gender and birthplace with numbers. I have also turned to the religion information. After several different schemes were thought up and discarded, I finally managed to classify the 31 types of religion listed on the data cards into five categories: R.C., Protestant, Other Christian, Jewish, and Other. I think this represents a small enough group to allow meaningful regression analysis. On the other hand, if I ever wish to disaggregate these groups, I have left the original variable of "religion" with 31 possible values in the file.

April 29

The other computer is gone, and most of my SPSS work is complete. I did not, however, finish the multivariate analysis. The reason for this was not the pressure of time; instead I had a computer problem. All the little bits of garbage produced by various programs had finally succeeded in shutting down the hard disc by writing over parts. Thus it was impossible to do anything else in SPSS. This left me at a convenient point to abandon statistical analysis. At the same time, I can always return to the subject, since my data files are on disc, and SPSS is available in faculty computer labs.

May 11

Now that the SPSS work is done, I have been concentrating on two things: revising "schoolhouse door" and writing "everyday life". This has led me to consider the point where the two papers overlap—the issue of oral testimony methodology. This is of course the subject of Ivor's work at present on the project, but it also interests me. When I met with Ivor earlier this week, he mentioned his interest in the "school days are the happiest days" interpretation of most of our subjects. He asked me to think about an explanation for this phenomenon.

It seems to me that two factors are at play here. First of all, part of it seems to be related to the way memories are stored. From what I understand of the working of the mind, most long-term memories are stored as analyzed pieces of information. That is, the brain first looks for patterns, or links to older information, before storing a memory. When the memory is invoked, the accompanying analysis comes with it. However, at the time of childhood memory storage, the individual probably has little in the way of a critical mind. When childhood memories are retrieved, they do not come with critical analytical interpretations. Such interpretations only arise when the subject decides to confront his or her memories in the light of latter experience. Secondly, it also seems that many people see choices made in high school as determining their whole career. Challenging the legitimacy of the educational experience thus translates as challenging the whole life experience, which most people are unwilling to do.

May 20

In working on my "everyday life" paper, I have come to realize how different my use of oral testimony in this case is from the way Ivor would tend to use it. I am using a large number of interviews to seek a common description of the day-to-day educational experience. I am discarding any memories that seem atypical, or influenced by events or factors not common to all students. Ivor on the other hand is very interested in the oral testimony of individuals as individuals. He is intrigued both by the self-delivered life story, and by the researcher's construction of triangulated life histories. While both of these are obviously "stories," so in fact is the history I am trying to tell.

May 26

I had a short meeting with Ivor yesterday, during which he proposed a final version of the Beal project. His view (which we are to keep under wraps for now) involves the presentation of different "stories" of schooling—histories, life stories, life histories, and case studies followed by an interpretive examination of the different stories, focussing on issues such as representation and the appropriation of data. I am in full agreement with this suggestion; it is in fact more what I expected when I first took this position. It allows me to participate in a project which includes substantive history work, but also moves beyond it, in areas which fascinate me, but about which I have little knowledge. As Ivor's assistant, I had expected to be doing some "riding on his coattails" in terms of theory; it seems that now this time has come. To me, this means I can now see the project as a much more balanced partnership. It's funny, Ivor told me last September or so that he intended to become a fully visible participant in the project around Easter or so. He's right on schedule. This is not to say that Ivor has not been contributing to the project; it is just that I could not see the results of most of his work in the earlier stage. I was just going on faith (as I have been doing with this journal). Now, that period is over.

June 25

It has been roughly a month since I last made an entry in this diary. That does not mean that I have not been working on the project. Instead it indicates something about the priority I set on this aspect of it. In the previous months, when I spent most of my time doing research, and little on writing, this diary was an interesting alternative task. Now as I concentrate on writing, the diary seems more of a chore. I think the problem involved is that my struggles with methodological issues now emerge in the writing of various papers, making any regurgitation of them here seem redundant. At this point, I am starting to think that a more useful methodological "diary" can be found in various drafts of our papers.

To summarise my work in the last four weeks, it has for the most part been a question of rewriting papers. I did, however, spend a week and a half finishing most of our first round of interviews. Only a couple of prospective interview subjects remain on our list.

July 3

I spent all of last Friday talking with Ivor about the project. Among the decisions we made was an outline of publications. It looks like we could produce up to four books (*ROP IV*, basically a collection of papers we have ready; two versions of "Telling Stories of School," one of them for academics and one for practitioners; and a full-fledged historical study of Beal to come out last). We also decided to consider Margaret Fallona as a subject for a life story or life history. We have to position the actual proposal. The key issue is how to emphasise one particular side of our intended undertaking—rather than the whole package—without crossing the line of misrepresentation.

August 18

Ivor has asked me to spend some time determining the feasibility of a newspaper search for the Beal school in the post-war period. We are thinking about asking a graduate student to undertake such a search. I started by checking out the possibility of existing clipping files at Althouse or the Board of Education. Althouse's library has clipping files dating back to 1965. They are not, however, organised by institution, but by topic. This is not in itself a serious problem, since every clipping file would be easier than reading every page of every issue of the newspaper. The problem instead concerns the coverage of the clippings; librarians only clip articles that deal with "issues," and ignore those which deal with more "ephemeral" subjects. This means that notices of extra-curricular activities, sports or anything that does not arouse controversy are ignored. I have in fact already examined all the files which seem most promising, and have only turned up a handful of articles dealing with Beal. I phoned the Board of Education to enquire about clipping files there. I spoke with someone in Tom Moore's office (I believe it was his executive assistant) who told me that their clipping files only started in 1986. She did promise, though, to talk to their librarian about any holdings their "professional library" might contain.

I also phoned Beal S. S., to arrange another look at their scrapbooks, in order to discover the extent of coverage involved. The new principal (Bruce Parker having retired) wanted to meet me in person, so I am meeting him first thing in the morning on Tuesday, August 25th. I hope to spend the rest of the day in the school archives.

Finally, I intend to spend a day or so examining a given year of the *London Free Press*, to determine the amount of information available, and the time it would take to extract it.

CHAPTER SEVEN

Conjunctures and Critical Incidents

Conjunctures

A good deal of recent work on educational change has sought to employ the concept of "conjunctures," key critical moments of change (see Goodson, 2005; Goodson and Hargreaves 2006). The concept of conjuncture is linked to the fundamental theoretical contribution of the Annalistes (Goodson, 2005), the understanding that the past is composed of different types of time (Henretta, 1979; Rinser, 1981). Though the definitions differ from author to author, the broad scheme posits three sorts of time—long, medium, and short—all of which are superimposed and interpenetrate. In long time are found trading patterns, geography, and the resource base. This is also the location of mentalités—long-term world view—the chief focus of most Annaliste history in the English language. At medium time are phenomena that go in cycles; mainly economic, but also sociocultural. As for events (and individual people), in Annaliste terms they are short-term phenomena with little meaning. According to its critics, in Annaliste history, people lose their individuality and act at the command of geographic or ecological determinism.[3]

Though some historians use *conjuncture* simply to describe medium-term phenomena, a second concept is more interesting; in this usage, *conjuncture* describes specific times when medium-term phenomena change and events interpenetrate. In Annaliste work, medium time is visualized as an arena of cycles and trends, some linked and some independent. These may be said to resemble a set of pendulums with differing periods, each dropping through the perpendicular at its own time. On rare occasions, many pendulums go through the vertical axis simultaneously. But even such times of widespread change are not totalizing: though many things change, some do not.

In some ways, the historical insights of the Annalistes are similar to the economic theories of Kondratieff (1984). He argued that the focus on short-term trade cycles meant that economists missed forecasting the major economic events—the economic conjunctures. These conjunctures came every sixty to eighty years and represented major economic restructurings where the ground rules of economic life were reformed and reassembled. If Kondratieff is right, and economic change follows these long cycles, we might expect that educational change follows similar patterns. The intersection between economic history and schooling is a substantially unexplored topic and in analysing conjuncture, it is imperative. It implies that substantial Kondratieff swings in the economy will be echoed by major conjunctures in the world of schooling.

Finding Conjunctures

There are two routes to identifying a conjuncture. First, you can approach the question by looking for an important event in the way described above and then seeing if it did in fact mark a conjuncture. A conjuncture provides actors with structures of opportunity. Once an important event has been suggested, analyse the trends at the other levels of time to see if the event did represent the seizing of opportunity. Of course, opportunity missed cannot be identified this way.

A second way is to work in the opposite direction, by identifying those periods when a conjuncture was possible. In this case, you have to decide what phenomena you see fitting into which type of time. Mindsets, trading cycles, and geography have traditionally been put into the category of long time and, thus, are unlikely to change in any study of recent educational history. Conjuncture occurs when several medium-term cycles enter coincidental periods of change. Thus, a way to search for conjuncture is to chart the medium-term cycles. Decide upon those cycles which are likely to have an effect on your chosen area of interest. These will be external to your school—operating at the level of local, regional, national, and international trends—in things such as curriculum reform, educational structures, or resource allocations, as well as more broad social and economic areas.

Conjuncture at Beal, 1968–1972. While interviewing people connected to Beal during the period from 1945 to 1980, we have found a consensus that the late 1960s and early 1970s marked a time of fundamental alteration. In the stories of former teachers and administrators, this change is usually attributed to the efforts of principal E.C. (Ernie) McTavish, who was in charge of the school during some of the most propitious times.

It does not surprise us to see an individual named as the prime mover of major changes; the story of Beal, as told within its walls, is the story of strong personalities: the original principal, Herbert Benson Beal; Maude "Mackie" Cryderman, founder of the art program; or Phillip J. Fallona, the long-time vice principal.[4] While respecting these narratives, we also want to look for other ways of describing the history of Beal.

"The times, they are a-changin." During the late 1960s and early 1970s, many of the organisational structures affecting Beal changed. While the language surrounding these changes seemed to reflect radical swings from previous endeavours, this masked the essential continuity of twentieth-century educational reform (Tyack, 1991). Most of these almost simultaneous alterations marked the next step in existing trends and cycles which had been going on for years or decades.

In June 1968, the Committee on Aims and Objectives of Education in the Schools of Ontario (the Hall-Dennis committee) published its report *Living and Learning* recommending wholesale reform of the provincial system to establish "a child-centred learning continuum that invites learning by individual discovery and inquiry" (p. 179), recommending wholesale reform of the provincial system. In the opinion of the standard history of twentieth-century Ontario schools, *Living and Learning* is "the most radical and bold document ever to originate from the bureaucratic labyrinth of the provincial Department of Education" (Stamp, 1982, p. 217).

Hall-Dennis created an atmosphere conducive to curriculum change at Beal. Teachers were taking the freedom implied by Hall-Dennis and trying new curriculum and new teaching methods—many of them having no direct relationship to the recommendations of the committee. One teacher recalled,

> It was a time, when I got there, there was a lot of experimentation going on. Hall-Dennis had just come in. And it was a very interesting situation because I don't think people really understood what Hall-Dennis was all about. And as a result, everybody was experimenting trying to find out what worked [Large interview].

This was especially true in academic subjects, where a typical, time-intensive project saw one class making a film remake of *Easy Rider* on London's streets (Large interview).

In the spring of 1969 came what was perhaps the most important direct result of Hall-Dennis—the introduction of a credit system, to which all high schools had to convert by September 1972. The credit system marked Ontario's turn to a subject promotion approach, applied not only to academic areas but for the first time, to vocational subjects as well. Under the new regulations, students needed to take a minimum of twenty-seven credits (each equivalent to 110–120 hours of class time) to receive a grade 12 graduation diploma. Of these twenty-seven, twelve had to come from particular areas (though students had some choice within the areas) and fifteen were totally elective (Gilbert, 1972, pp. 10–11). The credit system—made feasible by the ability of computers to do the time tabling—gave students a new degree of freedom in managing their secondary school career. According to proponents, it was intended to also give teachers greater autonomy in course design while allowing students to contribute to curriculum development through their choice of subject (Stamp, 1982, pp. 220–222).

The new approach had major repercussions on the schooling experience at Beal. For one thing, it marked the end of the system where a whole class moved together. In academics, this had led teachers to specialize the content of each class to accommodate students' practical interest. With the new system, each class had what older teachers thought a "peculiar mixture" of students from a variety of courses (Harper, interview).

"Teachers of practical courses found that the demand for course codes and definitions, with content written down beforehand, quickly stifled flexibility— the opposite effect from that which was promised" (A. Burns, interview, September 1994). For teachers in Beal's renowned art department, this meant more than just juggling figures to assign so many credits for majors and minors. It became much harder to introduce the sort of new ideas which had brought the school into national prominence (Fry, interview; Jefferess, interview; J. O'Henley, interview, June 1994).

The credit system also proved the end of the central concept of concentration in a specific technical area at the high school level. Under the old regime, technical students had taken a core speciality supplemented with strictly related areas—a route intended to lead straight to employment. Now students tended to pick a variety of subjects. As one teacher said,

> It monkeyed around with a system that I thought was working quite well, and it's pretty well destroyed it. (K. Leyland, interview, October 1994)

At the same time, the Ministry of Education, under the influence of the teachers' federation, tightened the rules for teacher qualification. Suddenly schools could get letters of permission allowing them to hire uncertified teachers only if absolutely no certified teacher in the province had applied for the job in question. Even when there was a pool of certified teachers, department heads lost their right to choose from them; they had to take whoever had the certificate and was next on the board's list (H. Ariss, interview; D. Irwin, interview).

This had special repercussions on practical areas. The art department had made its reputation in the 1960s on the teaching of practising artists, men and women who did not have teaching certificates. With the changes, no longer could the department head hire artists "off the street" (O'Henley, interview).

The new regulations also upset a cherished tradition in the technical departments of teachers handpicking their colleagues and successors from among former students working in industry and getting them into the teaching profession through Beal. This practice had marked a conscious attempt to ensure the transmission of certain values and approaches within the school (Irwin, interview).

The effects of these new rules were magnified by a series of trends which caused a large drainage of existing teachers from Beal. Many of these teachers went to new schools: In 1960, the Federal Technical and Vocational Training Assistance Act had inaugurated a boom in secondary school building and resulted in the construction of 335 new high schools in the province, as well as the funding of 83 expansions. To meet the requirements of the act, all of these schools and additions had to feature vocational education (Stamp, 1982). The job market for vocational teachers expanded widely, and prospects for advancement opened throughout the provincial system.

Other veteran teachers from Beal moved to administrative positions. In the 1960s, London's Board of Education went through a tremendous evolution; in this period of growth, it needed many more people at supervisory positions. At the same time, the idea that people who stayed too long in one place became biased and, thus, poor candidates for higher administrative positions, came into general acceptance. For prospective supervisors, it became a good career move to go through different schools (Rawson, interview).

Finally, some Beal teachers left the employ of the board to work in two new London institutions. Althouse College, the city's new teacher training institution, needed people to instruct the next generation of technical, commercial, and academic teachers, while the Ontario Vocational Centre (later Fanshawe College) offered postsecondary education in many of the subjects taught at Beal.

Another change in this period came with the weakening of the AVC. The AVC had supervised the operations of the school since its founding before the Great War. Reporting to the board of education, the AVC consisted of a varying number of trustees and appointees representing business and labour. As a distinct element in the city's bureaucracy, with wide powers regarding the school, the AVC ensured that Beal held a unique status in the city system. In practice, since many trustees and representatives spent only a few years on the committee, the school's early principals had been able to exert considerable power over decision making by the AVC—giving the principal at Beal much more power than his colleagues at the academic secondary schools in the city (T. Moore, personal communication; Rawson, interview). During the late 1960s and early 1970s, the unique status of Beal and its principal dissipated as the AVC took responsibility for several other schools and departments, funded under the Technical and Vocational Training Assistance Act, and lost a great deal of its administrative decision-making powers (London Board of Education, 1960–1970; London Board of Education [*Annual Report*], 1963, p.

13; Moore, personal communication). One additional trend, reaching a peak at this time, appears under a variety of names, including the youth revolt. By the last years of the 1960s,

> there were a lot of hippy types at Beal. I mean, if you didn't have hair to your shoulders, then you know, you weren't part of the crowd so to speak. It attracted that type. (B. Shaw, interview, February 1994)

Long hair and beards for men, and "frizzy hair" and miniskirts for women, were becoming the rule.

The new youth culture celebrated feeling over thought and sought ways to enhance the emotional experience, including drugs. The use of marijuana and LSD became common within school walls:

> The first floor was the entrance and the staircase. You could smell the marijuana sifting up.... Nobody seemed to care about it, the teachers didn't do anything to stop it. (B. Shaw, interview)

Students also turned to alcohol. The lowering of the legal drinking age to 18 (during the summer of 1971) made this more prevalent; lunchtime and afternoon drinking sessions became institutionalized in the student culture.

More than just dress and recreational habits changed. Student challenge to more fundamental school rules in this period reflected the larger assault being mounted by Western youth culture against the hegemony of those over thirty. In secondary schools, this vocal movement reached its provincial peak in late 1968 and early 1969, with a large-scale protest over the date chosen for the end of the school year and a three-week student sit-in at a Toronto high school (Stamp, 1982, pp. 225–228).

At Beal, the school's student newspaper, *The Word*, reflected the radical side of the youth movement. The issue for May 1969, for instance, opened with a satirical front page featuring a look at the school's latest "torture machines" under the slogan "If you can't beat a student, kill him." Inside, an editorial called on the student body to protest loudly and frequently against any perceived injustice, stating that a recent protest "showed the Department of Education that the Universities were not the only ones capable of raising a bit of trouble if pushed too far." The issue also included a full-page futuristic comic strip titled "The Revolution passed this way." In that episode, the hero—a London revolutionary named Alex—kills an evil "brain policeman" and heads for the life of a fugitive in the city's slums (*The Word*, May 28, 1969).

This new attitude also generated less dramatic, but more effective, agendas within the school walls. Students took an active role in determining the microstructures of their schooling experience. They sought to modify curriculum and pedagogy in the classroom. As one teacher put it, "They were testing, testing, testing all the time" (Large interview).

A Hero Emerges. Ernie McTavish, formerly a teacher of physical education and geography and principal at another London high school since mid-1964, came to Beal during the 1967–1968 school year. In January 1970, McTavish moved on to a supervisory position at the board office.[5] Though McTavish was only at Beal for a little over two years, he is credited with changing the whole environment of the school. For example, one interviewee said:

> "McTavish gave the students . . . a lot of rights. Freedom with responsibility was his philosophy" (D. Irwin, interview, March 1994).

Another observed:

> And then the big freedom came when Ernie McTavish became principal. And he unfortunately hadn't taught at Beal. He just was over there for a few months. He was a great guy. But, he sort of let the rules down and our kids just couldn't handle it. And this was about the time that the stupid government was lowering the drinking age. I had a grade ten class after lunch, and I'd have kids coming in drunk, sitting in front of me and falling asleep. They had too much freedom, too much at once. (P. Harper, interview, September 1994)

In the case of the students, McTavish's changes comprised a wholesale relaxation of the old rules of discipline. For an aging, negative system based on restrictions, he substituted a new set of rules with a positive emphasis on responsibility. For instance, instead of a total ban on smoking on school grounds, McTavish put out buckets of sand and let students smoke—if they looked after their mess. As he said at the time, "It seemed to me we were encouraging people to do things behind our backs. I wanted to bring things out in the open" (quoted in newspaper clipping, dated October 9, 1968, from school scrapbook; *LFP*, September 7, 1965; McLagan, interview; *The Word*, May 28, 1969).

Although a student had been suspended from Beal in 1965 for having hair which reached his collar, McTavish had no concerns with young men who chose long hair, although he did tell a student reporter that it might hurt them if they tried to get certain sorts of jobs (*LFP*, September 7, 1965; *The Word*, May 28, 1969).

Beyond his moves to liberalize structures for students, McTavish reconstructed the relationship between the administration and teaching staff. He gave teachers more input on policy decisions and explained more fully those decisions he made on his own:

He was good with the staff too. Ernie would give us a decision that had to be made, and the staff would discuss the various aspects, and the pros and cons and come up with a procedure. (McLagan, interview)

With a policy of support for teachers who sought to experiment in their curriculum or pedagogy, McTavish made the school "more humane, and more friendly" (McLagan, interview):

The respect for that man was just enormous. I think he sort of put his stamp on how the ship was to be run. He was the type of person who would give you your head if you had a good idea, and would let you run with it. He was into making things happen, or facilitating. (Large interview)

In this story, the departure of Vice Principal P.J. Fallona complemented the arrival of McTavish. After Principal H.B. Beal's retirement in the mid-1930s, Fallona came to be the central character in the school's historical consciousness. As principals at Beal changed more and more frequently, he spent a forty-year career behind its walls before retiring in 1969. The "heart and soul of the standards" at Beal, he would also, paradoxically, be the one in staff meetings trying to push other teachers to turn a 49 into a 50 (H. Rawson, interview, October 1994; see also B. Fry, interview, February 1994; C. Jefferess, interview, February 1994). Although an extremely fair man with a passionate commitment to learning, Fallona had always been stricter than his colleagues— even fellow teachers considered him "a hard old bugger" or a "martinet" (H. Ariss, interview, December 1990; V. Ritenburg, interview, September 1994). His leaving, then, provided a symbolic end to a particular era of Beal's history.

In the conclusion to this narrative, when McTavish left, his replacement sought to maintain the feeling of freedom but could not deal effectively with the new student behaviour and attitudes (Irwin, interview). Falling heir to something he had not started, the new principal's short tenure was marked by a prolonged period of strife; when he left shortly afterwards, the board of education replaced him with a man who insisted that staff and students stay within a strictly structured system (Ritenburg, interview).

Although a purely Annaliste reading of this period of Beal's history would play down McTavish's role completely, a more flexible interpretation makes him an important factor. Not every aspect of the school and its environment changed during the period from 1968 to 1972 (for instance, the basic organization of the school remained as it had), but enough did alter to create a conjuncture and allow an individual to influence both events and structures. In other words, structural change ensured that the loosening of old rules had to happen, but McTavish handled the situation well. He was "strong enough to handle it" (Irwin, interview).

As we know, the postwar economic settlement, fuelled by the rebuilding of the structures devastated by the war and by the baby boom, led to massive economic growth in North America. This period of economic expansion was echoed by a period of social change and experimentation, with many of the rules of social order being questioned and renegotiated. In the world of schooling, this conjuncture can be clearly traced in the collective memories of students and teachers at Beal. But in eliciting these traces, we should be aware that we are "keying in" to a major global shift in schooling regimens.

One of the clear messages for those studying schools in the 1960s is the emergence of heroic principals or at least in retrospect, of heroic principal stories. This can be evidenced in the innovative Toronto schools of the 1960s, such as Elgin Valley, but it is a widespread Western phenomenon. Smith, Kleine, Prunty, and Dwyer (1986), for instance, came across almost identical stories of a heroic principal who shifted the whole context of a school at the local level in St. Louis, Missouri, and of Tuula Gordon, who illustrated this phenomenon for Countesthorpe School in Leicestershire, England. At Beal, a similar heroic story emerges.

These principals were reacting to the opportunities suddenly offered by a new conjuncture in the world of schooling—in this sense, the stories offer us glimpses of structure. Macdonald (1991) has characterised sixties' schooling as distinctive for the "structures of opportunity," for as Barlow and Robertson (1994) put it,

> Relative prosperity, increased student enrolment, an aura of optimism and a culture of risk taking began to permeate schools. A sense of new possibilities was brought to classrooms by young and enthusiastic teachers, whose services were suddenly in demand. Early members of the post-war baby boom, these new teachers were unlikely to have led campus political protests, but neither were they completely untouched by the prevailing mood of challenge, change and political activism. (p. 5)

Our stories flesh out the responses to these structures.

Finally, whether or not one accepts the Annaliste approach, something important happened at Beal in the period from 1968 to 1972. The credit system, new rules about hiring teachers, McTavish's innovations, and student unrest all contributed to a period of change at H.B. Beal Secondary School. Like every other school in London, and many others across North America, the changes produced greater freedom for students. In the case of Beal, this came at the expense of the school's individuality. While the experience of being a "tech rat" changed radically, the school itself became much more than just one among many. Ironically, the introduction of a new, rigidly streamed curriculum at the start of the decade had been accompanied by a change in name; H.B. Beal went from a "technical and commercial high school" to a "secondary school," as did

London's academically oriented "collegiate institutes." It was, however, changes in the other direction which really blurred the lines between the two types of schools (London Board of Education [*Annual Report*], 1962, p. 16; London Board of Education [*Minutes*], 1962, p. 238).

CHAPTER EIGHT

Curriculum History

Beyond the overarching narratives of how schools develop in particular historical periods lies the fine-tuned details of each school's curriculum. By studying the history of a school timetable and the detailed curriculum guidelines and syllabuses that underpin the overall curriculum plan, a great deal of the detail of the life of a school can be exhumed and analysed. Curriculum history is therefore a vital tool for beginning to understand the life of a school. The field of curriculum history has grown exponentially since the 1960s, and a whole sequence of books now lay out how curriculum history has evolved in our schools. Beginning in 1985, Studies in Curriculum History[6] developed a wide range of studies of school subjects: classic science, domestic subjects, religious education, social studies, and modern languages. These studies reflect a growing interest in the history of curriculum and besides elucidating the symbolic drift of school knowledge towards the academic tradition, raise serious questions about explanations of school subjects. By studying curriculum history, scholars were able to discern not the overarching ideologies that underpin schooling but the fine-tuned details of how teachers and school students live their lives.

In the next section, a period of curriculum change is examined to highlight how work on curriculum history can broaden and develop our understanding of school life.

An Episode in School Curricular Change

The turn of the century was a time of turmoil in Canadian society. Changes in the economic organization of society had brought cultural assumptions dominant since midcentury into question. In Victorian times, the liberal, respectable professionals and their emulators had dominated cultural discourse in Canada. Now a new group took the reins of the middle class. Though by no means a monolithic group, businessmen, with their emphasis on efficiency, management, and scientific rationality, began to challenge the cultural discourse of the professionals. Their views could more easily coalesce with those of increasingly vocal subordinate groups. Women, workers, and immigrants could support, or be brought to accept, a new consensus which included—besides "business-like management"—social reform, domestic feminism, imperialism, and a combination of paternalism and coercion in industrial relations.[7]

Vocationalism—broadly, the idea that schools should prepare students for work and specifically, for industrial work—appeared as the educational component of this worldview. It brought scientific rationality to schools, while opening them up to the children of subordinate groups (Bowles & Gintis, 1976; Cremin, 1961; Kantor, 1988; Lazerson & Dunn, 1977; Lazerson & Grubb, 1974; Powers, 1992; Stamp, 1970). Vocationalism drew its theoretical support from the ideology of "social efficiency"—a school of educational thought which first emerged in the 1890s, taking inspiration from F.W. Taylor's theories of "scientific management." According to this approach, efficient schools should fit students for their future lives in the workplace and efficient educators should determine what the local society and economy need, find students most suited to these roles, and train them in their future functions, without any extra, useless education. Social efficiency supporters attacked the existing emphasis on university preparation in secondary schools as inefficient and alienating to the vast majority of students. Once in place, an efficient school system would contribute to a stable society, in which many of the new evils arising in the cities could be eradicated (Kliebard, 1986). Of course, the focus on dividing student bodies through special programs leading to disparate life outcomes demanded the sacrifice of individual equality of opportunity to the greater good of social efficiency. At the same time, the class, race, and gender bias built into the sorting process made vocationalism more appealing to some supporters of the existing matrix of schooling.

Social efficiency educational reform developed through a "coalition" of support. Three powerful constituencies have been discerned in the battle for vocationalism and social efficiency schooling at the provincial level and in London. Firstly, capital was represented by the Canadian Manufacturers Association, which was impressed with the potential of technical schooling to improve the productive skills of, and impose a form of institutional discipline on, the children of the working class. Yet it was also fearful that this type of schooling might reduce the distances between the social classes by expanding the opportunities of the working classes for socioeconomic mobility. Like their counterparts in Europe, the wealthy and the industrial and commercial bourgeoisie of Canada were willing to accept secondary schooling for the masses as long as it sharply distinguished between "liberal" and practical styles of schooling. This, they hoped, would have the effect of perpetuating and legitimating the social differences among classes through schooling, that is, exploiting the capacity of educational systems to invest social distinctions with "cultural meanings."

Reformers among the educational bureaucracy also supported the social efficiency theory, although they were far from in a majority. Their agenda differed from the manufacturers in quite distinct ways, as we shall see later. The educational reformers were concerned to obviate the status distinctions between vocational and academic schooling because they rightly saw that their career opportunities and material self-interest hinged on bridging this status divide. These educational groups tended to view the social efficiency movement as a new career opportunity and one with a promise of enhancement in personal and professional terms. Their concern, therefore, was to establish parity with academic forms of secondary schooling.

A third group was composed of organized labour, particularly as represented by the Trades and Labour Council. Organized labour, whilst extremely suspicious of the manufacturers, broadly supported the schooling which trained people in trades as long as it was placed under public control rather than undertaken privately in industrial organizations:

> The compromise among these three groups, the CMA [Canadian Manufacturers Association], the educators and the TLC [Trades and Labour Council], smoothed the way for the Industrial Education Act, passed by the Ontario provincial legislature in 1911. In brief, the Act authorised municipalities to establish a form of amplified schooling which complemented the already existing programs in manual training and domestic science at the elementary and secondary levels and commercial education in certain high schools. The most important feature of the Act was that it promised provincial funding for industrial education, enabling municipalities across the province to offer technical classes for adolescents beyond the school-leaving age of fourteen. (Goodson & Dowbiggin, 1991, p. 43)

In Ontario, those seeking to change education towards social efficiency ideals faced certain difficulties. Some members of the entrenched educational bureaucracy had not yet been won over by the move to business ideals. Instead, with individual exceptions, they clung to the worldview which had brought them their power—a worldview which tied directly back to Egerton Ryerson, the supreme Victorian authority in all matters educational (on Victorian education in Ontario, see Curtis, 1988; Gidney & Millar, 1990; Houston & Prentice, 1988). For more than a decade, supporters of vocational education waged a relentless campaign for reform (Stamp, 1970). Eventually, provincial and federal legislators, increasingly sympathetic to the calls for the efficient management of society, passed legislation which led to course realignment in a myriad of institutions, as well as the creation of dozens of new schools. While an important step, government funding for special programs and institutions did not represent the broad victory sought by the vocational movement.

The story of Herbert Benson Beal, and his struggle to reform education in London, Ontario, provides one detailed example from the struggle for vocational education. Beal joined the London Board of Education in the dying years of the nineteenth century; over the next decade, he worked his way to the principalship of one of the city's elementary schools and earned an administrative position at the city's Model School. The most crucial aspect of his career was his experience as a student at Teachers College, University of Columbia, where Beal encountered some of the leading lights in the new social efficiency movement (Goodson & Dowbiggin, 1991; Kliebard, 1986). At this time, Teachers College was a major centre for the teaching and promotion of social efficiency ideas, especially as seen in the work of David Sneddon.

Lobbied by Beal and like-minded supporters, the London Board of Education agreed to establish a terminal vocational secondary school in the city in 1912. For more than two decades, Beal, as principal of this school, under the nominal supervision of the ARC—a subcommittee of London's Board of Education and a body which Beal in fact dominated—possessed wide powers to introduce changes in the curriculum, in the public discourse of schooling, and in the institutional framework as it affected his school. The way Beal took advantage of these opportunities reveals both the ideological and the practical sides of his nature.

At the level of the classroom, Beal sought to emphasize practical work and to eliminate what he described as boring—and, thus, alienating—or simply unnecessary aspects of education. All students spent most of their time involved in practical subjects, which after 1921 included commercial studies. While Beal agreed with the necessity of teaching some traditional academic subjects, he instructed his staff to present them in a way related to the practical side of the curriculum. History lessons, for instance, should focus on the history of production. (London Technical and Commercial High School, 1925, pp. 7–8; 1933, pp. 6–7) Classroom teaching at the school remained committed to this sort of curriculum during the whole of Beal's twenty-three-year tenure as principal.

Beal departed from dominant norms of curriculum making in another way. He preferred to take his cue from local employers or workers rather than any self-proclaimed expert on curriculum. Before the establishment of regular courses, Beal frequently responded to groups of workers who requested classes in a specific aspect of their trade. As one example among many, in the fall of 1913, Beal approved new evening classes in theory of electrical work and sheet metal draughting on these grounds (AVC, 1913).

Beal continually emphasized this commitment to lay participation in curriculum making; in 1921, he said,

> It has been the policy of the school to invite suggestions from manufacturers, superintendents and foremen, especially those who come in contact with the graduates of our school. The greatest attention is given to their opinions in order that our courses of study might be strengthened and adapted as far as possible to actual requirements. (AVC, 1921, p. 55)

Three years later, he formalized this arrangement by appointing a "co-ordinating officer" who visited former students at their workplace to see how the training at the school could be improved by soliciting the opinions of the former students and their employers (AVC, 1924).

While Beal sought to introduce these changes to the secondary curriculum, he also challenged the existing emphasis on liberal education aimed at a professional elite. His rhetoric, drawn straight from the social efficiency movement, constantly emphasized that his school aimed at efficiently training carefully selected students "directly interested in Industrial occupations" (AVC, 1919, p. 125). Throughout his principalship, he maintained a continuous discourse of efficiency. The focus on efficient social goals is evident in such statements as the claim, in 1920, that "an analysis of the registration shows that the school is reaching the class of students to whose needs it is specially fitted to cater" (AVC, 1920, p. 167).

A decade later, Beal's reaction to the Depression illustrated his unchanged commitment to the doctrine of social efficiency:

> What should be the policy in times of depression like the present? It would manifestly be unwise to carry out the full placement program during such times. Care should be taken to distinguish between unemployment that is caused by the depression and technological unemployment, by which is meant the unemployment caused by the replacement of man-power by machines and mechanical devices. This latter employment will not return and schools should no longer prepare students for occupations thus rendered obsolete, but unemployment due to the general depression is temporary, and wisdom would dictate that we make careful preparation for the return of normal times. (*LFP*, May 16, 1933).

This attitude towards the school's purpose often set Beal's opinions apart from those of his more traditional colleagues; it meant, for instance, that Beal did not object to students quitting in the middle of their senior classes. In fact, he used figures for the destination of such students to claim aggressively that his school was doing its job, preparing students "for success in productive occupations" (AVC, 1922–1923).

This legitimating rhetoric not only emanated from Beal but also found reflection in the support of outsiders, of most AVC members, and of his teachers. Through the latter group of intermediaries, the social efficiency argument made its way into the viewpoint of the school's students, as notebooks and yearbooks illustrated. Thus one student, writing in the 1929 yearbook, claimed that the workforce makes two demands of a young man: that he be proficient enough in some vocation as to be of immediate value to his employer and that he has a general education which will allow him to become "a sane conservative citizen" (London Technical and Commercial High School, 1929, p. 8). (What the workplace demanded of a young women went unexamined.)

Besides challenging existing curriculum and rhetoric, Beal's school at first seemed to provide a clear example for social efficiency thinking which questioned the structural framework of secondary education. For most of the first decade of the London Industrial School's existence, its staff did not arrange "definite courses of study." Students were separated by gender but not by grade or major. Subject boundaries remained vague. The school also followed critical attacks on the social value of university preparation courses by offering none. In fact, this had played a crucial role in the school's establishment. A powerful segment of London's social and economic elite still maintained a "Victorian" worldview and supported the school because they saw it as a way of reducing crowding in the university preparation courses at the Collegiate Institute (Goodson & Dowbiggin, 1991). All the early proponents expected the London Industrial School to be a terminal institution preparing students for their lives in London's industrial economy.

Despite these beginnings, within eight years of the school's founding, its free and unstructured atmosphere had been replaced by all the traditional framework of grades, subjects, and courses. This new format included the subjects and classes that had previously been used as part of generalized technical and industrial courses; it also included a new university preparation course. The matriculation course was aimed at those students possessing high school entrance standing and intending to take engineering or domestic science at a university. The most noticeable innovations involved in this course comprised the addition of Latin and French to the subjects taken by technical students and the extension of the course of study to five years.

Did this represent a defeat for Beal? To find the answer to that question, it is necessary to consider curriculum change in a broader way.

On Explaining Curriculum Change

The addition of matriculation courses at Beal School provides an example of curriculum change which was at odds with the early "rhetorics of justification" for the school. Curriculum change which challenges foundational rhetoric is often associated with the power of "external constituencies." The notion of the power and influence of external constituencies or "publics" is derived from the work of John Meyer. In his work,

> external forces and structures emerge, not merely as sources of ideas, promptings, inducements and constraints but as definers and carriers of the categories of content, role and activity to which the practice of schools must approximate in order to attract support and legitimation. (Reid, 1984, p. 68)

Support and legitimation are often expressed through the existing patterns of structuration—in particular the way in which finance and resources are structured and allocated (Cohen, 1990).

The emergence and evolution of technical schooling, however, took place within an established "matrix" of schooling in London. A new, somewhat messianic initiative like Herbert Beal's was able to establish a new school, but the existing pattern of structuration provided a continuing logic of legitimisation. Meyer (1980) has commented on the strategic requirement of legitimisation if finances and resources are to be acquired and higher status achieved:

> The main problem for the administrator, if learning and participation are to be sustained, is to clearly link a particular educational organization or program to this wider institutional system. The school must be wholly accredited in everyone's eyes, or commitment and resources will rapidly decline. Ideally, it should be accredited as properly within a nationwide category of schools of general meaning and substantial allocation power—for example, it is better to be a college than a junior college, better to be a general high school than a vocational school, and so on. Much organizational activity must be devoted to maintaining institutional legitimacy. A stock of properly credentialed teachers is necessary, along with approved facilities and students who are themselves appropriately defined and credentialed. (p. 48)

Meyer argued that this pattern leads towards a conformity in the "categorical" categories of schooling:

> As a result, schools and curricula and courses tend toward isomorphism with national systems of categories. (p. 49)

The force of categorical type and the tendency for innovations to "regress" to the categorical norm can be illustrated in the case of Beal Technical School. Here we can see evidence of a school founded to pursue a vocational rhetoric of social efficiency but wrestling with the dominant system of status linked to academic "high schools." By 1918, Herbert Beal was beginning to realise the problems of status and resources which arise from innovation and categorical deviance. In an unpublished memo to the chairman and member of the AVC of the board of education, he noted,

> There are difficulties in the way of the school receiving the patronage of those who would profit from the courses provided that I should be lacking in my duty did I not bring them to the attention of the Committee at this time.
>
> In the first place you will recognize the fact that habit is one of the strongest motives in our lives and there is an educational habit in this Province that has been confirmed by generations. It has been the custom for boys and girls to proceed from the Kindergarten to the Public School, thence to the High School and thence to the University. It was the boast of our educational system that it led from the Kindergarten to the University. This time honoured habit is naturally followed by parents in selecting courses for their children in many cases without sufficient thought as to whether it is the most profitable course for the child to pursue. The problem is to induce the parent to select the course best suited to the needs of the child rather than to follow the custom referred to.
>
> The second difficulty is to bring the parents of the City to the realization of the true character of the courses of study provided in a Technical School. There is a popular idea that Technical Schools are for a class of more or less unfortunate pupils who are below the average mentally and that the courses judged from an academic standard are second class. Nothing could be further from the truth, but as long as this idea prevails the school will not receive the patronage it deserves. (AVC, 1918, p. 114)

Beal School in its early years was therefore suffering from its deviance from the established understandings of external publics: At a certain age, it was assumed that wherever possible, a child would progress through to the high school and from there to the university. This structure was a "time honoured habit," a traditional assumption.

Beal's dilemma therefore was to either defend its social efficiency vocational principles and risk marginalisation and a diminution of status and resources or find a way of joining the categorical type, the "high school." But to join the high school category inevitably meant joining the "matriculation" process. Curriculum change, it seems, was driven by the pursuit of resources and status, indeed, by the very need for institutional survival. As early as 1917, Beal had argued,

> No school can be managed economically without a sufficient number of students to allow proper classification. This is impossible with our present accommodation. In order to have one class of boys and one class of girls for first year both technical and industrial each of the size required to economically handle them in academic subjects we would require to have thirty boys and thirty girls with High School Entrance standing and thirty boys and thirty girls without High School Entrance standing. This is one hundred and twenty first year day students equally divided and this makes no allowance for shrinkage in the second year. This number could not be accommodated, but even this would leave no room for second and third year students. Classes of the same size in the second and third year are required to be economically carried on so that at the very least two hundred to three hundred students are required before anything like an economical classification can be made. At the present we have two academic class rooms provided for our use. You will see how impossible it is to economically conduct

a school with our present accommodation especially when the Education Department requires that teachers with specialist qualifications shall be engaged. (AVC, 1917, pp. 78–79)

By this time, then, Beal faced three interlinked problems, stated very succinctly in a 1918 memo:

> The problem of the organization of the work for the new building for September next presents three phases, namely: 1. What students will attend? 2. What courses of study shall be provided? 3. What instructors shall be secured? You will see that these questions are interdependent. The number and character of instructors required will depend on the courses to be provided and these in turn upon the number of students in attendance. The number of students will likewise depend on the character of the courses offered. Moreover competent teachers and instructors for Technical Schools are exceedingly hard to procure. They are required by Departmental regulations to have all the qualifications of High School teachers and in addition to possess such a knowledge of industrial processes and practice as to be able to correlate the academic studies with the practical work. Such a combination is not easy to find and such instructors cannot be secured on a moment's notice. It is therefore necessary that the question of the organization of the school should be considered with the greatest care and definitely decided upon as early in the year as possible if the school is to be ready for opening in September next. (AVC, 1918, p. 112)

Beal then goes on to itemize the kinds of students and courses he now thinks are required. For the first time, this includes the requirement of matriculation courses. Three kinds of day school courses are listed:

1. We may expect to receive boys and girls from the higher grades of the Public Schools [Canadian State Elementary Schools] to whose needs the regular Public School curriculum does not directly cater. These are more numerous than is generally supposed. We have it on the authority of the Education Department that our industries are recruited mainly from the boys and girls who do not go further than the sixth grade. This is a very serious handicap to the success of Canadian industries and to the life usefulness of the boys and girls who leave school so unprepared. By providing courses specially suited to the needs of these boys and girls their school life could be lengthened by from one to three years and their whole life career correspondingly improved. It was from the representation of the Superintendent of Education of this failure on the part of the Public Schools to hold boys and girls till they had received sufficient education to prepare them for a successful life career and useful citizenship that the Education Department decided to establish General Industrial courses in connection with Technical School.
2. The second class of boys and girls attending are those who now attend the Collegiate Institutes and High Schools but who do not propose taking departmental examinations or prepare for the learned professions other than engineering and technology. It has been the experience of principals of Collegiate Institutes and educationalists in general that there is a pressing need for special courses for these students who are not employing their time as profitably as they might under present High School courses. They should

be provided with a course which retains all the cultural value of the present High School course and combines with it a liberal allowance of technical work for boys and of domestic training for girls. In establishing these technical courses for boys and girls the question arose whether they should be given in Collegiate Institutes or in separate institutions, such as Technical Schools. The reasons for separating them were that while they were to retain all the cultural value of an academic course yet the technical work was of such importance and the whole course to fulfil its object, namely, to lead towards the higher directive positions in the industries, required distinctive courses. The teachers moreover, even of academic studies, must primarily have an interest in and a firsthand knowledge of industrial conditions. The mathematics must be applied rather than demonstrated. The science must have direct application to industrial processes which could hardly be expected in an institution conducted primarily for cultural courses. The atmosphere of the courses must be such as to create an attraction towards and respect for industrial occupations. For these reasons technical courses in separate institutions for this class of students are advisable.

3. The third class of students attending should be boys with High School Entrance standing desirous of obtaining matriculation for the School of Practical Science and girls with the same standing desiring matriculation for the Household Science Departments of the University and those desiring to prepare themselves for higher technical institutions of University standing. A regular matriculation course combined with special draughting and mathematics courses and special home economics courses for girls should be provided for this class of students. (AVC, 1918, pp. 112–113)

Beal's strategy for course redefinition and curriculum change appeared, then, to be a response to two major problems he was encountering. Firstly, the limited and specific type of student the school was attracting, which derived from "the popular idea the Technical Schools are for a class of more or less unfortunate pupils who are below the average mentally." Secondly, and associated with this problem, the obvious difficulty Beal was having in acquiring properly qualified teaching staff. Beal's response to these two problems, which threatened the very survival of the school, was clearly stated by 1918:

> The Education Department has insisted that the qualifications of teachers for Technical Schools shall be equal to that of Collegiate Institutes and the courses of study while different in character are in no way below the standard of Collegiate Institutes. It is indispensable to the success of your Technical School that it is placed on an equality with other schools in the estimation of the public. (AVC, 1918, pp. 114–115)

As we have seen "the public" had a view of high schools as an academic "categorical type" leading on to university. Hence, to have any claim to the high school category and to "equality of estimation," Beal had to develop matriculation courses. Hence, curriculum change resulted from a desire for "parity of esteem" and equality of status, resources, and finance.

Beal's memo of January 31, 1919, states the problem clearly:

> There will be a number of important problems to be considered by the Committee during the year. The first of these will be the ratification of the length and character of the Classes of study. The arrangement of permanent courses of study was impossible under the conditions obtaining in the old Building, but should be definitely decided and a proper Calendar of the School issued this year. In order to do this, and from the fact that most of the progressive younger teachers in the Province are teaching on Interim Certificates, which are made permanent by successful teaching experience in a School approved by the Educational Department, it is therefore of importance, if the School is to attract to its staff, the most desirable teachers, that it should receive the standing of a Technical High School. (AVC, 1919, pp. 132–133)

He therefore recommended

> that the Board of Education be requested to make application to the Department of Education for the school to be given the standing of a Technical High School. (AVC, 1919, pp. 132–133)

Hence, Beal finally seals the campaign to join the categorical type of "high school."

Beal and the AVC had been expecting the Department of Education to confer official high school status on the Technical School in the fall of 1919, a gesture that would have enabled the school to offer matriculation courses for students who wished to attend postsecondary faculties of engineering and domestic science and, hence, improved its chances of enrolling students who might otherwise attend the Collegiate Institute. Yet the Department of Education hesitated to approve the measure because the new headmaster who served under Principal Beal supposedly did not have the proper qualifications for his position.

Manning, chairman of the AVC, wrote to protest about the delay. Manning's letter coaxed the Department on October 7, 1919, into approving the Technical School's new headmaster and the school became the London Technical High School (Goodson & Dowbiggin, 1991).

Thus, Beal and his allies had to accept external definitions of institutional categories if they were to seek the resources that accompanied legitimacy; this did not, however, negate the whole social efficiency thrust of Beal's campaign. Though Beal did not do away with what some supporters of social efficiency saw as an irrelevant set of traditional structures, he did ensure that these structures supported his other ideals. In the new London Technical High School (granted that status in late 1919), Beal was supreme, his own status having been raised, as principal of a high school. Thus, when Beal and the AVC considered establishing a printing department, they undertook the following tasks:

> We have considered the local need for training boys to enter the printing trade, have visited the printing departments of other vocational schools, have consulted those engaged in the local trade, both as employers and employees and have considered the value of such training as a department of the present Technical High School course. (AVC, 1924, p. 36)

When the committee came up with a planned course, they submitted it to a "representative meeting of employers and employees of the printing trade in the City" for approval (AVC, 1924, p. 36).

Another piece of evidence supports the notion that Beal had little real commitment to the hegemonic structure he had accepted. If the changes of 1918–1919 meant more than a simple accommodation to prevailing methods of legitimisation, then the centrepiece was the establishment of a university preparation course, which took its first students in September of 1919. Yet in reality, over the next two decades, few students took the program and few completed it. To start with, no more than 10 percent of the first-year class of a given year enrolled in the matriculation course (see Table 1). A very low rate of success exacerbated the initial lack of size. Each year saw a wholesale decrease in the matriculation class through transfer, quitting, and failure.[8] With this sort of attrition, the upper classes remained tiny. In 1924, the combined size of the third- and fourth-year classes in the matriculation program was only twenty-three students (AVC, 1924). Obviously, Beal and his staff saw no reason to try to boost participation in this option.

Conclusion

What are we to make of these episodes in the evolution of the school which now bears Beal's name? Looked at from the viewpoint of Beal's original ideals, the end result seems an uneasy compromise. His school became a mix of socially efficient curriculum and rhetoric, resting ultimately on an "inefficient" traditional framework. Yet a closer look leads to the impression that Beal, while certainly an idealist, was also strategically sophisticated. Beal accepted the cultural and political necessity of the traditional framework; he accepted that the rhetoric of justification had to include both social efficiency and institutionalized categories, despite the inherent contradictions.

Beal's actions seem to support Meyer's (Meyer, 1980) argument that it is easier to change some aspects of educational systems than others. In particular, institutionalized definitions of matters such as courses, types of students, or subjects are the most resistant to change. Beal, like other reformers, realised that the educational bureaucracy still maintained a high degree of control over the framework of schooling, if not over the actual practice of teaching. While

Beal did not challenge the traditional structures, and indeed took advantage of them, he did make the changes which would have the greatest effects on the education of his students. As an informed actor, knowledgeable about some of the constraints upon him, Beal managed to achieve significant victories in building up his school programs, in attracting resources, and in acquiring status for both the teachers and the school.

Curriculum change, then, is embedded within wider patterns of structurisation and strategic contestation. To understand the intentions of curriculum redefinition, it is necessary to both explore the internal micro politics of the school and the external manoeuvrings for institutional and political legitimisation. Each curricular change serves to reflect the mediation between internal and external milieu and to signify historic compromise according to the conditions of time and place. As such, curricular inquiry might best be conducted through sociohistorical investigation—a form of investigation that has to date been somewhat underrepresented in a field that has too often viewed curriculum study as a mode of technical-rational implementation. Hopefully, through historical study, we can approach the complexity of the underpinning social and political process.

APPENDIX 1

London, Ont.,
May 19, 1919.
Present:
W.N. Manning
H. Hayman
W.A. Reid
Mrs. A.T. Edwards
A.E. Silverwood
W.J. Tillman
R. Lawson
H.B. Beal

A letter from the Minister of Education, dated April 7th, 1919, in reference to granting to the school the standing of a Technical High School, was read.

Moved by Mr. Silverwood, seconded by Mr. Lawson and carried that the Secretary be instructed to notify the Minister of Education as follows:

"That the conditions stated by the Minister of Education in his letter of April 7th, requiring the appointment of a teacher as headmaster of Day Classes who holds a High School Principal's certificate and who is approved by the Minister in order to give the school the rank of a Technical High school be accepted; it being understood that the Minister requires that the headmaster of Day Classes shall be responsible to the Department of Education, to the Advisory Industrial Committee and to the Board of Education through Principal of the School and that the Principal of the School be held responsible by the Department of Education, the Advisory Industrial Committee and the Board of Education for the policy and management of the School." That if necessary, the Chairman of the Committee interview the Minister of Education in regard to the matter.

Moved by Mr. Hayman, seconded by Mr. Silverwood that the Principal be instructed to advertise for a Science Specialist with High School Principals qualifications, the salary to be up to $2500 according to experience.

The design for the tablet to mark the official opening of the School was submitted by the Dennis Wire & Iron Works Co. Moved by Mr. Hayman, seconded by Mr. Lawson that the Chairman and Principal be empowered to place order.

APPENDIX 2

October 7, 1919.

A meeting of the Advisory Industrial Committee was held in the City Hall at 4.15 this afternoon. The following members were present: Messrs. Silverwood, Lawson, Udy, Barnard, Manning, Mrs. Edwards, R.M. McElheran and H.B.B.

On motion the report of Mr. Manning was adopted:

TO THE MEMBERS OF THE ADVISORY INDUSTRIAL COMMITTEE:

I would report as follows:

That during the month the Chairman of the Board received a communication from the Department in regard to the standing of the school as a Technical High School.

I communicated with Dr. Cody and he sent Dr. Merchant to finally settle any misunderstanding. Dr. Merchant arrived this morning.

I discussed the resolution of the Advisory Industrial Committee of May 19th with him and found that he quite agreed with the resolution of the Advisory Industrial Committee as we understood it, but so that there should be no possible misunderstanding he suggested that the resolution be worded as follows and this being done the Department, on receiving notice thereof, would grant to the school the standing of a Technical High School:

"That the conditions stated by the Minister of Education in his letter of April 7th, requiring the appointment of a teacher as headmaster of Day Classes who holds a High School Principal's certificate and who is approved by the Minister in order to give the school the rank of a Technical High School be accepted; it being understood that the Minister requires that the headmaster of Day Classes shall be responsible to the Department of Education through the Director of Technical Education and the Principal of the School and to the Advisory Industrial Committee, and to the Board of Education through the Principal of the School and that the Principal of the School be held responsible by the Department of Education, the Advisory Industrial Committee and the Board of Education for the policy and management of the School."

I would therefore advise that the resolution as worded be passed and sent to the Board for ratification.

Sgd. W. N. Manning
Chairman,
Advisory Industrial Committee.

Table 1. Percentage of Students Entering First Year of a General Course, at Four-Year Intervals.

Year	Technical (%)	Commercial (%)*	Matriculation (%)	n
1919	90.9	—	9.1	55
1923	54.4	35.2	10.4	270
1927	37.1	58.1	4.8	105
1931	49.5	43.3	7.3	386
1935	61.1	32.6	6.3	720

*Commercial courses were not offered in 1919.
Source: London Technical and Commercial High School Student Record Cards, H.B. Beal Secondary School Archives.

CHAPTER NINE

Studying School Subjects

Patterns of Gender and Class

The concept of subject status used in this chapter emerges from a definition used by researchers dealing with the status of individuals; this definition sees status as deriving from ownership of and control of access to material and symbolic capital (Bourdieu & Passeron, 1977; Deever, 1990; Labaree, 1988). Subject status essentially represents the collective professional status of subject teachers (Goodson, 1995, 2005; Goodson, Anstead, & Mangan, 1998). Its material side may consist of remuneration in cases where teachers in different departments receive different salaries. It can also cover career prospects, which may increase, for instance, when a subject earns departmental status. The material capital of a subject also consists of the collective resources in terms of buildings, classrooms, and equipment which determine the working conditions for subject teachers. The symbolic side of subject status includes the authority or respect accorded to the subject, as well as the extent to which it controls access to a form of knowledge deemed valuable. This knowledge can be described in terms of cultural capital or credentials; its value reflects the degree of desirability of the opportunities for future prospects opened to the subject's students (Bourdieu & Passeron, 1977; Deever, 1990; Giroux & Penna, 1983; Labaree, 1986, 1988; Ringer, 1987; Short & Waks, 2009). This chapter further argues that in the early twentieth century, a discipline's symbolic capital derived partly from the perceived value of the student body and could change as a result of transformations in student socioeconomic characteristics.

Commercial studies, which moved from the Collegiate Institute[9] to London's technical high school in 1920, underwent a major curriculum revision in the middle of the decade; as a result, the commercial course evolved from a single common general course into three courses of different lengths, with different emphases, aimed at different groups of students. The discipline had already experienced one major change at the start of the decade, when the Provincial Department of Education ordered its extension from two to three years. According to Principal Herbert Benson Beal, this allowed students to train for "the higher positions in mercantile life" (AVC, 1922, p. 4). At the same time, the school allowed students the choice of leaving after two years with a "junior diploma," which Beal described as adequate preparation for "junior and stenographic positions" (AVC, 1924, p. 3).[10] At this point, though, all commercial students enrolled in the same general course. The first major exception to this rule took the form of a one-year "Special Commercial" course created in 1924. This course admitted only those students who already had several years of secondary school experience. It served to attract dozens of young women (and smaller numbers of young men) who had finished their academic education at one of London's prestigious academic schools—styled as collegiate institutes—or in a few cases, other schools. Because these students had already obtained a grounding in academic subjects at their previous school, the special one-year course featured only strictly vocational classes (AVC, 1925, p. 3; M. Fallona, interview, 1990; London Board of Education, 1924, p. 77; London Technical and Commercial High School Student Record Cards, H.B. Beal Secondary School Archives).[11]

In 1926, the school announced the formation of a "Special Business Course for Boys," which became a "General Business Course for Boys" in 1933 (London Board of Education, 1926–1933). This new course had a different focus from the general commercial course; while the older course trained students to take general office positions, the new course trained male students for positions at wholesale firms and financial institutions or in sales. As Beal pointed out, the course would prepare young men to work in places where they could find "ample opportunity for advancement" (AVC, 1927, p. 7; 1928, p. 3).[12]

Why did these changes come about? One obvious hypothesis, that the provincial government insisted on their introduction, does not fit the evidence. Certainly, in both cases the provincial department allowed or authorized these changes, but they did not demand them. It was a purely local decision to take advantage of these options, and one which Principal Beal seems primarily to have made. Neither the local board of education nor the AVC—which oversaw the school's operations—urged Beal in this direction; instead, they simply reacted to his decisions (AVC, 1920–1930; London Board of Education, 1920–1930). On the other hand, a lack of documents makes the question of whether Beal felt some pressure from commercial teachers in the school unanswerable, though that seems a reasonable contention.

Why did Beal (probably acting in conjunction with commercial teachers in his school) decide to introduce these courses, and what interests did they serve? If the new courses were to serve the interests of the students, then they should have changed the school experience in some way. In fact, the two innovations did little to alter existing practices. The special commercial course did not change anything for students at the technical school since they could not take it. Instead of making improvements for an existing student clientele, the course sought to attract another group of students. Had this new group consisted of young people who would otherwise have left the educational system, the change would have represented a laudable attempt to build on the school's original mandate. The new course, however, did not seek out the otherwise unschooled but instead, aimed at attracting educated youths away from private business colleges or even from the collegiates.

On the other hand, the creation of separate courses for males only marked the public confirmation of a pattern that had existed for years. From the first years of commercial courses at the technical school, the classes had a slightly different curriculum for each gender. The new course promised an emphasis on penmanship, business correspondence, accountancy, investment math, and salesmanship; yet the male classes in the general commercial course already featured more of an emphasis on accountancy than did those for females. The existing separate classes in other subjects for each gender would have allowed for an emphasis on penmanship, business correspondence, or investment mathematics if desired. The only real change in curriculum came with the introduction of a class in salesmanship; the introduction of a brand new course was primarily a feat of legerdemain (London Technical and Commercial High School Student Record Cards, H.B. Beal Secondary School Archives; see also N. Jackson & Gaskell, 1987, p. 192).

The existing gender differences in curriculum fit into a wider pattern in the school (and, of course, wider patterns beyond the school); although all Ontario schools were premised on the American model of coeducation, female students at the technical school followed a different curriculum from males (see Goodson & Dowbiggin, 1991).[13] Besides the obvious differences in the technical subjects taken by each gender, males at the school took algebra throughout their course, whether they had entered a general technical, matriculation, or general commercial stream, while only those few females enrolled in the matriculation course took algebra, and they only took it from second year. In the technical department, females took art but males did not (London Technical and Commercial High School, 1921).

Since the two new courses in no way responded to student demands, they seem to have been created mainly for the educators themselves. Commercial teachers did have definite occupational concerns at the time. In particular, they faced a clear decrease in the status of commercial studies, which occurred during the period from the turn of the century to the 1920s.

During the late nineteenth century, commercial studies managed to amass substantial symbolic and material resources in the Ontario school system. From midcentury, classes in such business subjects as bookkeeping and penmanship became standard in the province's secondary schools. As demand for this sort of professional training grew during the second half of the nineteenth century, private business colleges proliferated, emphasizing a purely practical curriculum and guaranteed placement for graduates. The Ministry of Education also responded to this demand, introducing a one-year commercial course in 1885 and extending it to two years in 1896 (N. Jackson & Gaskell, 1987, pp. 186–187).[14]

In London at this time, commercial subjects made up part of the general academic curriculum at the city's Collegiate Institute. Commercial studies commanded increasing authority and in 1895, became a separate department, with a distinct course of study, at the Collegiate Institute. In 1899, the commercial department moved to a new four-room building adjacent to the older Collegiate Institute building. From that point on, reports of attendance at the school listed students in the commercial department separately (Dickinson, 1935, pp. 7–8; London Board of Education, 1898–1899, pp. 25–26, p. 38, p. 87). Both of these actions point to an acknowledgement of the amount of symbolic capital controlled by commercial education at the end of the nineteenth century; departmental status provided material resources in terms of additional teaching positions up to and including department head, while the new building represented a high standard of working conditions. Indeed, the incoming chair of the London Board of Education confirmed this status in 1899 when he declared the primary role of the local system to be the provision of "a good English and Business education" (London Board of Education, 1899–1900, pp. 2–3).

The success of commercial studies in the late nineteenth century reflected the association of office work with middle-class male respectability. Middle-class men in the late nineteenth century viewed clerical work as the first, obligatory, rung on a ladder of commercial success. Young men who wanted to make up the next generation of merchants, bankers, or entrepreneurs knew they had to serve their time as clerks, bookkeepers, or secretaries. Many educators, worried about the movement of young women into the high schools, saw commercial courses as a way to make school more relevant and attractive to these male students (Gidney & Millar, 1990, p. 294; N. Jackson & Gaskell, 1987, pp. 182–183).

Although the achievement of departmental standing, and quarters in a new building, resulted from commercial studies' high status at the Collegiate Institute, the physical and administrative separation from academic subjects made the department much more vulnerable to marginalization as its cultural authority decreased during the opening decades of the twentieth century.[15] At this time, the symbolic capital associated with the value of the subject dropped throughout North America; thus, the 1900 annual report of the Ontario Minister of Education quoted the opinion of the president of Harvard

University on commercial courses, which he saw as "hopelessly inferior to other courses" (N. Jackson & Gaskell, 1987, p. 193).

The physical resources which contributed to the status of commercial studies reflected the subject's large enrolment at the turn of the century; a province-wide decline in enrolment in the early twentieth century accelerated the decrease in subject status. In 1902, 11,334 students in Ontario secondary schools took bookkeeping among their subjects. By 1922, that number had fallen to 6,524. The increase in absolute enrolment made the relative decline in the attraction of commercial studies even greater. Almost half (46 percent) of Ontario's secondary students took bookkeeping in 1902; twenty years later, the proportion had fallen to less than 15 percent (Ontario Minister of Education, 1922, pp. 260–263).

In London, the decline in commercial education's status led to marginalization, beginning early in the new century with the establishment of domestic science classes in the commercial building, thus reducing the material resources controlled by commercial teachers. Domestic science classes were held in the commercial building from 1903, and by 1907, the commercial building had become too crowded (London Board of Education, 1902–1903, p. 44, p. 52; 1907, p. 196). In 1908, the "severe overcrowding" had reached the point where one commercial class consisted of sixty-two pupils sharing eleven typewriters. Some of the pressure eased later that year with the transfer of domestic science classes to the basement of the main building (London Board of Education, 1908, pp. 315–316, p. 355). The commercial building remained crowded as it aged, and teaching conditions worsened. In 1915, the principal reported an average class size of forty-nine, despite provincial regulations limiting class size to thirty. By that point, the principal was talking of "separating the Commercial Department from the rest of the Collegiate work" (London Board of Education, 1915, p. 53, pp. 130–131).

After the end of the war, overcrowding at the commercial building reached a crisis point. In 1918, the board authorized the removal of a staircase, so classes could be held in a hallway, and the creation of a new classroom in the attic (London Board of Education, 1918, p. 140). Finally, in 1919, the board decided to act. At first they considered a new building in a site distant from the Collegiate Institute since in their opinion, "it would be preferable to have the Commercial Classes entirely separated from the Collegiate Institute" (London Board of Education, 1919, p. 53). When the city council refused to allow the funds for this, the board decided to move the commercial classes into an old, decrepit, elementary school building used by the military during the war; academic classes would move into the former commercial building. Even these poor quarters did not provide immunity for the commercial department; in September of 1919, academic classes which could not fit in the other two buildings took over one of the department's six classrooms (London Board of Education, 1919, pp. 84–85, pp. 134–135, p. 138, p. 141, p. 183).

The transfer of the commercial department to the London Technical High School in the early 1920s represented another stage in the subject's downward trajectory. The technical high school had a remarkably different status from the Collegiate Institute, a difference based in the symbolic rather than the material realm. One of the chief factors behind the formation of the "London Industrial School" (later the "London Technical and Commercial High School") in 1912 was a desire to ease overcrowding at the Collegiate Institute by the transfer of students who only attended the school for a year or two before entering the industrial workforce. Enthused by the claims of the movement for social efficiency, London educators undertook the implementation of a school which would prepare these students for their expected careers (Goodson & Dowbiggin, 1989, pp. 43–44).[16]

Thus, from the start, the technical school suffered under the image of an institution for less desirable students. The school's first principal, and prime mover in its creation, Herbert Benson Beal, did not take this complacently; instead, he fought to raise the public's estimation of his school by attracting students who had achieved high school entrance standing. Beal wanted to challenge and in the end, destroy a widespread perception of technical schools as the natural dumping ground for all backward and defective children

The willingness of both federal and provincial levels of government to fund technical schooling handsomely at this time provided an important boost to Beal's campaign and brought control over considerable material resources to the school. The construction of a brand new building (completed in 1918) filled with up-to-date equipment seemed to signal Beal's complete victory, and caused many traditionalists, led by the *LFP*, to attack the technical school on a variety of issues, all underpinned by a feeling that this new form of schooling presented a serious challenge to the cultural dominance of traditional elite academic education (Goodson & Dowbiggin, 1991, pp. 47–56).

The last of the campaigns of opposition took place in 1923 and early 1924. This campaign started with a series of attacks by the newspaper and council members which maligned the school in terms of its standards of teaching. Opponents also described the school as an inefficient part of the local system, claiming that it was too expensive and too little used (*LFP*, December 29, 1923; January 2–9, 1924; February 5, 1924). The climax of this campaign came with a movement to convert the technical school into a comprehensive high school, combining academic and technical streams. While this would have prevented the resulting school from challenging the Collegiate Institute on status grounds, it also promised to eliminate another problem—the growing need for some kind of secondary school in the city's predominantly working-class East

End. The combined weight of technical education supporters, spokespeople for the East End community who wanted their own collegiate institute, and provincial officials opposed to the comprehensive plan finally scuttled this movement (*LFP*, January 29–February 8, 1924; London Board of Education, 1924, p. 26, pp. 41–43).

Despite victories like this, and the early burst of funding from provincial and federal sources, any increase in status experienced by the technical high school proved short lived. Neither of these factors led to any great increase in symbolic capital since the key distinction between practical and academic forms of knowledge remained firmly in place. In 1926, the board eliminated all the manual training and domestic science classes from the city's collegiate institutes (by that point the city had three collegiate institutes), making the distinction between these schools and the technical school more sharp (London Board of Education, 1926, pp. 350–352).

Despite Beal's efforts, his school remained starved of symbolic capital. A teacher who arrived at the school in 1930 remembered how a "general feeling" existed "that you were rather an inferior type if you attended Beal Tech. It was for the people who just didn't have the ability or didn't belong to the right class of people." Or put another way, "if you weren't very bright you went to Tech. And [you also went] . . . if your family was poor" (Fallona, interview; Mann, n.d.).

In 1920, this technical institution, burdened with continuing status problems, became the new home of the commercial studies department formerly associated with the Collegiate Institute. The destruction by fire in April 1920 of the Collegiate Institute building only hastened the implementation of existing plans to move the commercial students to the technical school. Within days of the disaster, administrators worked out a new arrangement; academic classes from the burned-out building moved into the classrooms occupied by commercial courses, and commercial courses moved to the technical school building. Though the commercial department remained administratively connected to the Collegiate for several months, the move proved permanent; the commercial department became an official part of the technical school a year after the fire and emergency move (Dickinson, 1935, p. 8; London Board of Education, 1920–1921). Commercial education, once a highly respected component of the Collegiate Institute curriculum, had now been consigned (along with domestic science and industrial education) to the technical school building.[17]

In 1924, facing this situation of declining status, commercial educators embarked on a set of curricular changes to increase the material and symbolic resources of their department. They had the full support of Principal Beal, constantly concerned with his school's status, which had been seriously threatened in the previous eighteen months. One way to increase the material resources of the discipline was to increase enrolment, resulting in a greater number of paid positions available to teachers of the subject and a greater voice in the distribution of other material resources. The provincially ordered expansion to a three-year course in 1921 had certainly contributed in this vein, but such an increase in bodies seemed to have little effect on symbolic wealth. The reforms initiated at the middle of the decade, by contrast, aimed to increase material resources, with more students and more courses, but they also evinced a concern with symbolic resources through the recruitment of new student clienteles. This underscores the beliefs of the educators involved that student characteristics had an effect on subject status.

Taking the second reform first, the creation of a gender-segregated course represented a reaction to the observation that commercial classes, like commercial work, had become dominated by females. A perception that this fact had negative status implications caused commercial educators throughout the continent to seek some means of redressing the balance. Many business teachers sought to model their subject on the increasingly prestigious professional schools, which laid a heavy emphasis on masculinity; the presence of a female student body seemed to threaten this goal (Weiss, 1978, pp. 176–177). Of course, such concerns were unique to neither commercial studies nor North America.

In the twentieth century, the respectable and male aura of commercial studies started to diminish as more and more positions for women opened up in clerical work. The Canadian economy underwent great changes in the generation surrounding the turn of the century. A fairly sudden transformation from entrepreneurial to corporate forms of capitalism meant the volume of clerical work increased, and offices became the central directing agencies of huge economic entities. In an effort to rationalize these new phenomena, and maintain power in the hands of managers, clerical tasks became specialized and routinised. The new positions did not call for a few generalists with a wealth of skills but instead, for various specialists with limited skills; thus, they paid poorly and offered little chance of advancement. These jobs did not suit the aspirations of most males entering the business world, but they did seem a step above traditional female paid work as a domestic or factory worker; female clerical workers flooded into the Canadian office in the first thirty years of the twentieth century (N. Jackson & Gaskell, 1987, pp. 184–185; Kantor, 1988, p. 62; Labaree, 1988, pp. 166–168; Lowe, 1986). By 1931, women held almost half of all clerical jobs in the country; over half of these women worked as typists and stenographers. In these junior positions, women outnumbered men by a ratio of more than twenty to one (Canada, 1931, vol. 7, p. 74).

Commercial education itself changed in reaction to these transformations. The addition of new subjects like stenography and typewriting around the turn of the century showed a curriculum adaptation to new circumstances. The commercial student body also reflected this new reality; by the time commercial education was widely and successfully established in the province, the majority of students enrolled in such courses were probably female. Young women ignored the wishes of mainstream educational reformers, who proclaimed the merits of domestic science, and eagerly sought the training which prepared them for the flood of new clerical jobs.[19] In an unpublished study, Gail Posen (1980) found that women outnumbered men by a ratio of three to one in Toronto's High School of Commerce from 1911 through to the Second World War. In 1930, the six strictly commercial high schools operating in the province all reported a similar dominance of female students, who made up over three-quarters of the 6,721 students enrolled at those institutions (Ontario Minister of Education, 1920, p. 250; 1925, p. 216; 1930, p. 352). These figures tie the Ontario experience to that of American schools which also saw a female majority in commercial classes appearing in the first decades of the twentieth century (Ontario Minister of Education, 1930, p. 352; Powers, 1992, pp. 113–127; Rury, 1984, pp. 30–33; Weiss, 1982, p. 627).

London was not immune to these provincial, national, and international trends. Increasingly in the twentieth century, women took jobs in the city's clerical workforce. A comparison of the census figures for 1911 and 1921 provides a small illustration of this movement. In 1911, London's banks employed 121 male clerks and 20 female clerks, while its insurance offices employed 53 male and 36 female clerks. By 1921, the number of male bank clerks had increased by only 1, and the number of male insurance clerks dropped by 24; over the same period, the numbers of female bank and insurance clerks increased by 81 and 82, respectively. Twenty years later, 2,393 held commercial positions in London (Canada, 1911, vol. 6, p. 340; 1921, vol. 4, pp. 432–434; 1941, vol. 7, p. 238).

At the same time as women became a fixture in London's offices, their younger sisters started to change the matrix of local secondary education. From the start of the new century, girls frequently outnumbered boys at the Collegiate. Many of them ignored the domestic subjects, introduced to the local curriculum in 1902 (London Board of Education, 1902–1903, pp. 5–9, p. 52). Instead, they chose to take commercial studies, leading to a female dominance in the subject. Commercial studies had certainly become feminized by the time the program came to the technical school in 1920. A list of commercial diplomas awarded by the school in the first year of commercial studies included twenty-eight female names and only six male names. In 1923, the group of students entering the first year of the commercial program numbered 71 young women and only 19 young men (London Board of Education, Report, 1921, p. 89) London Technical and Commercial High School Student Record Cards, H.B. Beal Secondary School Archives; for data from 1927 and 1929, see Goodson & Dowbiggin, 1989, pp. 32–33). A similar ratio continued to mark the commercial program through the next two decades. In 1930, the number of students enrolled in commercial classes included 462 young women and 105 young men. In 1940, the school awarded eighty-five intermediate certificates in commercial studies, of which seventy went to young women (*London Board of Education Report,* 1940, pp. 72–73; Ontario Minister of Education, 1930, p. 353).[20]

The possibility that this female influx had major repercussions for subject status resides in the nature of gender roles and relations at the time. In education, as in so many areas of early twentieth-century life, the experience of London's women and girls differed markedly from that of the city's men and boys. A wealth of evidence supports this interpretation at the level of the board of education and, especially, at the level of the teaching staff; it must have held true at the level of the students.

Women in London had little representation on their board of education—the locally elected body which supervised the city's schools. Although one female trustee did serve a single term at the end of the nineteenth century, women only started to achieve sustained representation on the board from 1919. Though the 1920 board included four women out of fourteen trustees, for the next few years the board included only one or two women at a time. In 1928, the board reduced itself to six members. The number of women members on this board stayed constant at one or two until at least 1940. Women trustees took another important step with the election of the first female chair of the board in 1929, followed by two more women in that office in 1933 and 1934. Although the representation of women on the board did increase over time, it never reached an equality with that of men in this period, despite the fact that both streams of feminism—maternal feminism and equal rights feminism—had an interest in education. One of these pioneer female trustees reflected the prevailing denigration of women's experience when she concluded her report of an annual convention to the board by regretting that no male trustee from the city had attended the convention and adding, "My report is only from a woman's viewpoint" (London Board of Education, 1920, p. 93). The deadpan delivery of sixty-year-old minutes prevents us from listening for any trace of sarcasm.

Female teachers experienced vastly different professional lives from those of their male colleagues. As in other places, London's female teachers faced discrimination in terms of status, both through official decisions on things like salaries or promotions and in the general level of treatment they received. A definite and formal gender differentiation appeared in the salaries paid teachers. As an example, the 1932 salary schedule for the London Board of Education paid female elementary school teachers with a first-class certificate a maximum of $1,800 a year, while those with a second-class certificate could receive up to $1,600; the corresponding maximums for male teachers stood at $2,500 and $2,400, respectively. The terms for teachers in secondary schools were more equal, but a formal difference remained; thus, teachers in the highest category received $3,400 a year if male and $3,200 if female (London Board of Education, 1931, appendix). Of course, this latter statistic had little meaning for the majority of female teachers, clustered at the elementary level.

In terms of promotion, women could not move above the level of classroom teacher. Technically, the board did allow female principals in schools containing less than eight rooms, but in practice this meant that one teacher in each of the schools (only two operated in 1928) which had only two full-time teachers received the title of principal, with little increase in pay or status (London Board of Education, 1923, pp. 43–51; 1928, pp. 30–34). In the secondary schools, women could not become a department head outside of the female technical subjects (Fallona, interview; London Board of Education, 1915). Advertisements for job openings always sought candidates in terms of gender; the board ignored any women who applied for a male job unless they could find no suitable man. One teacher recalled her experience at being hired during the Depression: "They wanted a Commercial specialist, they wanted a man; but apparently they couldn't get a man, so they took me" (Fallona, interview; London Board of Education, 1921, p. 201).

Simply stated, school authorities treated female teachers as second-class employees. The board expected female teachers who married to give up their positions, and would only consider hiring a married woman, even for a substitute position, in an emergency (Fallona, interview; London Board of Education, 1933, p. 58). When a chair of the board of education spoke in favour of introducing mandatory retirement, he saw no problem in suggesting that men retire at 65 and women at 55 years of age (London Board of Education, 1905, p. 95). Of course, this all took place in a society that by and large took such things for granted. Many female teachers themselves felt it was simply logical that men have higher pay, that only men became principals, and that women should drop out when married and turn their attention to raising a family (Fallona, interview).

The creation of a special commercial course for boys in 1926, then, represented an attempt to alter the slide in subject status through the recruitment of a more socially valued student clientele; did it succeed? Did the introduction of the course actually change the gender split in the subject? The answer has to be negative. Table 1 outlines the gender division in new commercial students, taking all commercial courses into account, at four-year intervals. Despite the introduction of the new course in 1926, males made up roughly 20 percent of new commercial students in 1927 and 1931, as they had in 1923. It is only in 1935 that even a minor change in ratio is detectable.

Table 1: Percentage of Students Entering First Year of Any Commercial Course, by Gender

	1923 (%)	1927 (%)	1931 (%)	1935 (%)
Male	21	20	21	24
Female	79	80	79	76
n	91	325	292	406

Despite the apparent failure of the new course to significantly alter the gender ratio in the commercial department, it still may have helped with the symbolic status of the discipline, since the mere presence of this course on the books provided evidence for commercial studies' importance. In an attempt to raise the status of commercial classes generally, the staff at Beal pointed to gender differences in education and in particular, to the presence of young men in segregated classes. By contrast, the school did not refer to other commercial courses as being "for Girls," indicating the low status of a female clientele, and leaving the impression that all commercial courses contained some males.

While the introduction of a specifically gender-segregated course reveals an obvious attempt to manipulate student characteristics, the introduction of the special one-year course demands closer inspection. In fact, the special commercial course also sought to attract a new group of students—students with a different socioeconomic background from those normally associated with the technical school. The move of the commercial department to the technical school (a result of the decrease in status associated with the gender characteristics of students) had started a further round of devaluation associated with the socioeconomic background of pupils; gender and class patterns began to interact in a vicious downward spiral. In the 1920s and 1930s, new patterns of attendance brought about by legislative and economic changes tied technical schools more and more firmly to a working-class student body perceived to have less academic ability (N. Jackson & Gaskell, 1987, pp. 193–194; see also Kantor, 1988, pp. 123–148).

The composition of London's technical school's student body differed dramatically from that of the more academically oriented Collegiate. A comparison of the occupational status of student families at the Collegiate Institute and the technical school shows this discrepancy. Table 2 reveals that two-thirds of the pupils in the Collegiate came from families headed by men or women employed in white-collar positions, while only one-fifth of technical school pupils came from this group. The figures for manual occupations are reversed.[21]

Table 2: Parental Occupations, London Secondary Schools, 1922

	Collegiate Institute (%)	Technical High School (%)
Nonmanual	66.3	21.5
Manual skilled	30.1	58.2
Manual unskilled	3.6	20.3
n	880	423

Source: Ontario Minister of Education (1922, pp. 228–229, 260–261).

Once established at the technical school, commercial studies drew from its pool of students. Table 3 identifies student socioeconomic status on the basis of the parental occupation listed on student record cards from the technical school. This table reveals the similarity in the socioeconomic status of students in the two general courses. The data show that a slight difference in class characteristics of female students taking the general technical and commercial courses existed in 1927 but vanished thereafter. For 1931 and 1935, the patterns of representation seem almost identical. Thus, at least in the 1930s, class had no bearing on patterns of enrolment in the two general courses, and commercial studies, thus, suffered the double disability of a student body undervalued both in gender and in class terms.

Table 3: Socioeconomic Characteristics of Female Students in Selected Courses

	General Technical (%)	General Commercial (%)	Special Commercial (%)
1927			
Nonmanual	19	30	53
Skilled manual	40	36	28
Unskilled manual	40	33	19
n	67	129	58
1931			
Nonmanual	25	24	39
Skilled manual	37	38	42
Unskilled manual	38	38	19
n	92	105	69
1935			
Nonmanual	30	33	60
Skilled manual	33	35	30
Unskilled manual	37	32	10
n	81	135	83

Source: London Technical and Commercial High School Student Record Cards, H.B. Beal Secondary School Archives.

The special one-year course sought to remedy this problem. Because the course demanded at least two years of high school standing for admission, it enrolled only students who transferred from another secondary school, which meant in practice usually one of the collegiate institutes, though a few came from private schools or rural continuation schools. Many of the students entering this course had already achieved junior or senior matriculation; in a few cases, young women even attended this course after graduating from university (Fallona, interview; London Technical and Commercial High School Student Record Cards, H.B. Beal Secondary School Archives; P. Morgan, interview, June 10, 1989 [Morgan taught in the technical school at the time]). The special commercial course thus drew students not from the general pool of students entering the technical school but from a pool of those who had entered the collegiate institutes or other secondary institutions.

The presence of the new group of students changed the socioeconomic composition of the commercial department. Table 3 shows how the socioeconomic status of these students contrasted with that of the students in the two general courses discussed above. Where the nonmanual segment of the general courses varied between one-fifth and one-third of all students, in the special commercial course it varied from two-fifths to three-fifths. At its minimum, it still exceeded the maximum for either of the other two courses.

These two new courses, then, emerged at the technical school to help raise teachers' professional status; while doing so, the courses also increased lines of segregation within the student population based on ascribed, involuntary characteristics. The creation of a course restricted to males added to the formal distinction between the genders in school society. The special one-year course produced similar, if less obvious, effects. While the new course did succeed in attracting a more highly valued clientele, in doing so it created a new division in the student body, which corresponded to a difference in socioeconomic status.

While the class-based segregation imposed by the new course did not upset proponents of social efficiency, it did mark an unintended, if acceptable, outcome. Although Beal himself did attempt to minimize the social distance between the special commercial pupils and those from the general courses by organizing school-wide recreational activities (Morgan, interview), these social events did nothing more than mask the systematic stratification being worked at the level of curriculum.

As is so often the case in historical research, the authors have to wonder whether their edifice of argument and evidence appears to others as little more than a house of cards. Direct evidence supports the following assertions. First, during the period 1900 to 1920, commercial studies in London, Ontario, suffered from a trend of increasing marginalization in the Collegiate Institute, which culminated in a transfer to the technical high school—an institution with a much less enviable reputation. Second, this marginalization occurred at the same time as the subject's student body underwent a process of feminization. Third, at the technical school, the commercial studies student body quickly became identical, in social class terms, to the technical student body and different from that of the Collegiate Institute. Fourth, during 1923 and 1924, the school underwent a series of attacks led by the conservative local newspaper and city council members. Fifth, soon after these attacks ended, school officials decided to introduce two new courses which made little difference to existing students. Sixth, the first of the new courses aimed to attract collegiate institute students and resulted in a different class composition in the student body. Seventh, the other new course aimed at attracting males and, thus, directly sought to change the student body profile.

This chapter tries to tie these seven phenomena together in one particular and specific sense by arguing for the importance of the notion of subject status. Since subject status played a major role in determining professional career status and prospects, the personal interests of commercial teachers demanded attempts to elevate the discipline's status. One way to do so involved changing the characteristics of the student body, since at this time subject status rested to a degree on the perceived value of the students enrolled. In particular, student social characteristics of gender and class acted as crucial determinants in setting the status of a particular subject. The curriculum change of the mid-1920s sought to achieve this restructuring.

In the end, the struggle for professional status resulted in a major increase in stratification and segregation in the technical school. While educators acknowledged the gender segregation, the more circumspect class segregation provided similarly potent mechanisms for structuring student experience in the school. The result was a distinction by class and gender in the credentials students received from their secondary schooling. The fact that these changes took place under provincial authority seems to indicate that London's situation was far from unique and might have reflected a province-wide concern with the status of commercial studies. This suggests strongly that the 1920s witnessed increased socioeconomic segregation in secondary school commercial courses throughout Ontario—a conclusion which matches recent interpretations of the so-called vocational era in the history of education (see Kantor, 1988; Kantor & Tyack, 1982; Labaree, 1988; Lazerson & Dunn, 1977; Lazerson & Grubb, 1974; Powers, 1992).

CHAPTER TEN

Studying the Everyday Life of a School

In 1992, Harold Silver noted that the history of education pays little attention to students and their experience, especially at the level of the classroom. The following description of the day-to-day experience of schooling, as it took place at London Technical and Commercial High School between 1920 and 1940, is our attempt to answer at least part of this challenge. The construction of such pieces might seem to be simply description—something that history professors tell their freshest undergraduate students to avoid. Yet Annaliste "total history," Foucault's "genealogies," and postmodernism's emphasis on letting other voices speak all seem to indicate some intellectual support for the future of "history as description." At the same time, such an approach bridges the gap to popular culture's construction of "history."

Beyond this, a description of the commonplace practices of a typical day at a particular school allow glimpses of the underlying structures and mediating practices of educational experience. As Giddens (1981, 1984, 2011); Bhaskar (1979); and Baumann (2001) have pointed out, structures are constituted by human social practices, often institutionalised practices, which they themselves have shaped. The human actors are always knowledgeable about some of the conditions of the surrounding system, though the consequences of their action may be unforeseen. Structures both constrain and enable practice so that all structures offer some institutional space for transformative action.

The work of Giddens (2011) and Bhaskar (1979) provides a theoretical foundation for researchers seeking to reconstruct the everyday human actions which contribute to the maintenance—or downfall—of a social system predicated on an uneven balance of power. In some cases, the more extreme structuralism present in the work of Giddens and Bhaskar has led to an interpretation of everyday life and practices as merely the "superficial" consequences of underlying factors. For instance, Cooper (1985) argued in his study of mathematics curriculum practice that "observed events and their correlations are the superficial consequences of underlying structures and relationships" (p. 6).

In this chapter, we take a more dialectical view. We see institutionalised practices and social structures and relations as mutually constitutive. In the context of a school case study, these ideas lead us to consider the relationship between structures and institutionalised practices within the school, as well as the role of the various sorts of people implicated in these practices.

Sources of evidence for these pieces, in order of importance, will likely be 1) oral testimony, 2) photographic evidence, and 3) school timetables and similar administrative documents. You might consider sending your piece out to some of your interview subjects for their response.

This use of oral testimony is very different from life history work. You are using a large number of interviews to seek a common description of the day-to-day educational experience. This means discarding any memories that seem atypical or influenced by events or factors not common to all students. Life historians, on the other hand, are very interested in the oral testimony of individuals as individuals. They are intrigued both by the self-delivered life story and by the researcher's construction of triangulated life histories.

Glimpses of Everyday Life at London Technical and Commercial High School, 1920–1940

Each day at the London Technical and Commercial High School started with the arrival of the students. In wintertime, most would travel to school on foot, many of them walking several miles a day. In better weather, flocks of bicycles appeared as the day started. For those students who lived near its route, the Street railway provided an easier means of travel—it stopped just outside the school. Finally, a handful of students arrived by car. Few families in London had an automobile and only a minority of them had one which a teenager could take.

The teachers arrived in much the same way. Many walked, while most of the male teachers, at least, rode bicycles in suitable weather. Some teachers arrived on the Street railway, while a select few brought their automobiles.

When they arrived at school, students congregated outside their assigned external doors, with boys at one end of the school, and girls, almost a block away, at the other—starting the daily segregation of the genders. A different segregation also took effect: students could not use the central front doors, which were reserved for teachers and office staff (for comparison, see Sutherland, 1986, p. 178). As they stood around, students took care to stay off the grass lawns in front of the school; even cutting across a corner of the lawn served as grounds for a reprimand (Geddes, interview).

The students all arrived wearing their "school clothes," which they had to take off when they returned home; the same dress or shirt and pants might be worn for several days in a row before going into the wash. For boys—whether in commercial or technical programs—proper dress included dress pants (often of worsted wool), sweaters, shirts, and ties. In the 1930s, some of the specialized technical students wore more appropriate clothing, such as denim overalls for motor mechanic students (Cushman, interview). For girls, a dress or skirt was normal. For much of the period, an unofficial female uniform predominated, with girls wearing navy blue pleated skirts and "middies"— white blouses trimmed with sailor's collars (Stamp, 1975, p. 68, notes the same "uniform" in Calgary).

After entering the school, students moved to their lockers to discard coats and drop off some of their books before reporting to their homeroom. Every homeroom contained roughly forty students, which represented one class in the commercial side but comprised two classes of twenty students each for technical students. Each class sat in alphabetical order. After conducting a roll call, the homeroom teacher made up a class list which one student carried from room to room until midafternoon, when he or she dropped it off at the office. This gave teachers in each subject a chance to add any comments until that time (Hopkins, interview).

Until the fall of 1928 (when a school auditorium was built), the completion of the morning roll call signalled the commencement of the first class of the day; in the years after that, a different order was followed. After the roll call, the students left their books and moved down to the auditorium for morning exercises. The whole school went in; each class had their own place to sit, though members of the school orchestra scurried to their pit ahead of the others and struck up their polished version of *Finlandia* or some similar piece (Brooks, interview). On a typical day, the assembly would feature the royal anthem, a hymn or two (with the words projected onto a screen), prayers, school announcements—concerning both official policy and extracurricular activities—and, perhaps, a short speech. Principal H.B. Beal—a short, red-headed man, who favoured "English" vests and tweeds—often took the duty of leading this assembly, which frequently was the only contact a student had with the principal. According to one student, Beal "wasn't a big guy, physically, and his voice wasn't very big either. It's a wonder that the words got to the back of the auditorium" (Brooks, interview).

Normally the auditorium session lasted for some fifteen or twenty minutes, but on occasion, generally about once a week, the assembly lasted for an hour or longer and featured different kinds of educational entertainment. After the assembly, the students returned to their classroom and started the day's lessons—some of them remaining in their homeroom while others collected their books and headed elsewhere.

At this point in the day, the sharp distinction between commercial and technical students became apparent. Very little mixing took place between commercial and technical students. Even nonvocational classes, such as academic subjects or physical training, were taken separately.

The subjects which students took during the school day had, for the most part, already been chosen by the administration; students rarely had any options. This meant that the same group of students remained together as a class for the whole day. To assign students to a class at the beginning of the year, teachers in each course divided their students by gender and then lined them up alphabetically. They would then count off the required number for each class. In some cases, the leftovers from each gender would be combined into one class, which then sat with the boys and girls separated in the classroom. Each class moved as a group from room to room in single file, while the teachers stayed in their own rooms. In the classroom, each student sat in the same seat all year long, generally in alphabetical order. In commercial studies, the same group tended to go though the whole three or four years together, while in technical studies, specialization changed class composition after first or second year.

For most students, the particular subjects that they took depended on the course and year. In first year, for example, students in the technical side's three-year general course received an introduction to the range of specialities available. Thus, young men in the 1921–1922 school year took classes in woodworking, machine shop, electricity, building construction, and draughting.

The young men entering first year would be expected to produce a variety of standard projects in each of these subjects. One early machine shop project started as a piece of cast iron, five-eighths of an inch thick and about three by four inches. Students first drilled three-eighths inch holes in the corners and then drilled a number of connecting small holes in the middle until they could drop the centre out. Next they had to trim the piece in the shaper. The teachers had some students do this drilling and shaping in the opposite order, so that not all were waiting for the same machine.

Students then moved on to the second project; they had to turn a piece of iron in the lathe. The piece of iron, of course, was just a round piece, eight or nine inches long and about an inch and a half in diameter, which you first of all had to drill a centre hole in each end, and then put it in the lathe and turn it smooth, to a set diameter—for which you were checked and marked. And eventually it ended up as a piece which had a taper on it and you put a thread on it in the lathe. (Hopkins, interview)

Students had to complete this second project in time for the Christmas break. Along the way, students also received more didactic training, in the form of delivered lessons, reinforced with blackboard notes, on such things as sharpening tools, the proper use of tools, and the names of the various parts of their tools (Hopkins, interview).

A typical shop class would number fifteen to twenty students under one teacher, who spent most of his time going from pupil to pupil to check their work. The layout of the technical department frequently meant that two such classes would share a room. In this case, the two teachers involved would work together, though the work of each class remained distinct. The two classes might each use a separate part of the shop room, divided by "an invisible line" (Hopkins, interview). Such team teaching was a common feature of technical education at the school. In many cases, the two teachers had complementary strengths, with one teacher having a stronger teaching background and the other having more practical experience in the industry.

For their second or third year, male technical students picked one subject in which to specialize. Students who had picked a specialization generally spent roughly half their time in the subject, at times taking trips to relevant local industries. Technical students also took some academic classes.

The projects of the senior students were, by reason of specialization, much more complex than those of first-year students. Indeed, the projects were frequently much more "practical" in the sense that they attended to the needs of the school itself: for example, students in woodworking built all the teachers' desks; printing students provided all printed material the school needed, from standard forms to report cards and even school yearbooks; electricity teachers assigned specific students to keep a close eye on the backup batteries used for the school's emergency lighting system; other electricity students ran the lighting for school assemblies and evening events; and all senior students and teachers were ready to pitch in and repair any piece of school equipment which broke down.

The motor mechanics classroom had a seating area, but most of it comprised a shop, practice engines, workbenches, and a huge tool room. The tool room operated under very specific rules, as one student recalled:

> We had all the tools in a big tool room; every week ... one of the students was assigned to the tool room, and he was in charge of tools. I mean you'd go for tools and there was a board and your number—you had six tags on each peg. Say my number was 26, well there'd be six "26" tags there. Now, if I wanted some tool they'd go and get me my tool and hang my tag where they took the tool off, and that was the way they'd keep track of it. And we never left there at night, until every tag was back on that board. If there was a tool missing, the whole class was looking for it. (Walsh, interview)

At first students learned on practice engines. When the teacher felt they had mastered the basic skills, they would be allowed to work on real cars—cars sent by teachers, students, or their families, who received free repairs, except for the cost of parts. Students in the auto course used a current automotive repair manual, from one of the major manufacturers, as a textbook. They studied it from cover to cover and even had homework assignments based on it.

Draughting took place in three rooms on the third floor, including a small blueprint room and two rooms with draughting tables. Draughting courses usually started with students each receiving an article, such as a spindle table leg. Each student had to measure the article, make a quick hand sketch, and then produce a full-size draughting blueprint.

In the printing shop, the first lesson involved learning how to set type, as well as how to find type in the special print job cases:

> On the very first day, you were supposed to set the type for your name, your Street address, and the city. And then go over and ink the form, and put a piece of paper in and roll it off. And you were marked on that. (Hopkins, interview)

The woodworking shops, on the second floor, featured lots of machines, including half a dozen wood lathes. In first year, each student had the same project; they had to learn to use a hand plane, saw, and chisel on wood—mostly straight hand work. The department bought rough lumber, which they stored in a special area, sometimes used to teach students about materials. Some wood went into a small room with a steam radiator for drying it out (Hopkins, interview).

The electricity department consisted of three rooms: a store room, with switchboard and engines; a lecture room with lots of chalkboards; and a third room containing a wooden structure, representing a building under construction, which was used for practice wiring. When the framework became too filled with holes, woodworking students would rebuild it.

While boys in the technical courses went through these areas, female technical students studied domestic subjects. In these domestic classes, teachers taught cooking and sewing skills, and spent a lot of time discussing efficient methods of housekeeping, including particular dusting, sweeping, or floor washing techniques.

Sewing class featured various forms of needlework: sewing, crochet, embroidery, and petit point. The students' first projects usually involved making petticoats and lampshades. Some teachers had to improvise:

> We all couldn't afford knitting needles at times, and [the teacher] went to Anderson's butcher shop by the market and got us skewers that you put in meat, and string, and that's what she taught us on. (Brown, interview)

The school provided three rooms on the third floor for the cooking side of domestic science. Each had a couple of big stoves, along with gas burners for each student. (Later they were replaced by electrical burners.) The teacher would announce the day's work, give a demonstration, and then depending on the teacher, either sit quietly at the other end of the room or roam from student to student. In season, students would learn to can peaches. They also made lots of cream soups—"not what you would cook for a working man" (Darnell, interview). The class members seemed to spend a great deal of their time cleaning up.

One special course taught in the technical side—the only one open to both male and female students—was art, taught by Mrs. Cryderman, a flamboyant figure "known for her hats" (Carter, interview). Although her class emphasised the fine arts, Cryderman taught more commercial applications, such as sign painting, as well:

> She taught... silk batik work, don't recall that we did watercolour work, which was not my forte. But I don't recall using oils. For the first year it was a lot more varied crafts really than, in conjunction with art. Like the silk batik work. And she was good at all of those things. And of course we did life drawing, with these plaster casts, we didn't have any nude models then. (Carter, interview)

Art students also took technical subjects, such as sewing and dressmaking for the young women, as well as basic draughting.

In contrast to the variety of trades taught in technical courses, commercial courses focused on three subjects: typing, shorthand, and bookkeeping. Passing the year depended on adequate speeds in typing and shorthand, so classes involved a lot of drills and tests for speed. One typing teacher encouraged his students to type to music, using a given piece, instead of a stopwatch, to time their work (Allison, interview). Others used blindfolds on their students (Brown, interview). Procedures and type of equipment were all as up-to-date as a typical office of the time, though the typewriters were allowed to age before they were replaced. Students also took lessons in skills such as filing and could earn special certificates in these skills, sponsored by various office supply companies (M.F., interview).

Commercial students also took rapid calculation—a special course on techniques for adding columns of figures. The teacher who taught that subject had a tendency to start his classes somewhat abruptly, as one student recalled:

> Of course, when we'd get to his room, we'd all start to talk, naturally.... He carried a three foot ruler and he'd come in that back door and bang that on the wall and just about scare us out of our wits. (Smith, interview)

This teacher spent many classes in speed tests, with students required to add a column of figures in a given period of time. His habit of banging his pointer to mark the halfway point caused some students to jump and completely forget the sum they were carrying in their heads (Cull, interview).

Teachers in this course also offered lessons on proper office etiquette. Women in the commercial courses were taught to be quiet and listen. They were not taught to be aggressive or independent, qualities not welcomed by employers of female office help (M.F., interview; Geddes, interview;).

The same group of teachers taught academics to pupils from each section of school. Most academic teachers put the day's work on the board and then went up and down the aisles to check each student's progress and often, to confirm that they had done the assigned homework. If teachers wished to include any additional information as part of the lesson, they delivered it in the form of a lecture while standing at the front of the room. The walls of the classroom tended to be very bare, with just the blackboards and a picture of the king and queen (compare to Stamp, 1975, p. 62; Sutherland, 1986, pp. 183–184).

Homework was considered very important at the school; students got homework every night and the load increased as exams got closer. These exams took place at Christmas, Easter, and in June and covered academic subjects as well as theory related to practical subjects. Students had to pass every subject; those who failed one—vocational or academic—failed the year.

An account of one teacher's math classes illustrates the highly structured pedagogy often practiced. Each day, this teacher would start by sending ten students (of the twenty in the class) to put their solutions to homework problems on the blackboard. Those who did it one day knew they would not do it the next, since he alternated the same groups of ten all year. However, if the teacher thought certain students had not done their homework, then he might send them to the board on a day they were not expecting it. This teacher spent the whole period on his feet in this manner and then ended the day with new homework assignments. While sticking with this very structured style, the teacher tried to make the content interesting. Thus, he used baseball scores and players' statistics as a way to teach mathematics to his class of senior boys, requiring his pupils to bring in the scores from the paper each day (Hopkins, interview).

Not every teacher followed this plan; the English teachers in particular tended to employ a different teaching style, inviting class discussions, which sometimes led to "pretty hot arguments" (Walsh, interview). Yet even in this case, most of the teaching came from the front of the room, though one particular teacher preferred to move to the back of her room.

Students in English class spent a lot of time reading out loud or reciting memorized passages. They generally used modern translations of Shakespeare, along with other British works—George Eliot, Sir Walter Scott, and collections of the standard poets. One student described an English teacher this way: "She used to make books come alive. She would give us all a part and we'd have to act it out" (Richardson, interview). Another teacher also encouraged his students to immerse themselves in Shakespeare's plays, having some of the boys fence with yardsticks at the front of the room. At times he did the acting himself, running into the hall, pounding on the classroom door, and then rushing inside to recite "The Highwayman" (Mitchell, interview).

Some academic subjects were taught with content considered more relevant to technical or commercial students than what the collegiates taught. Both maths and sciences were taught from special texts aimed at technical schools:

> The physics was geared [towards] mechanics, and they went into far more detail on mechanics than they did in the collegiates. I think we had more on gearing and pulleys and inclined planes and wedges and so on, more experiments and so on, which was geared to our future work situations. (Mitchell, interview)

The content of the first-year history course in the mid-1920s also reflected this impulse. The course started with civics—first studying local government, then the provincial government, and finally federal institutions. That took from September to December. In the next term, students studied the history of industry, which culminated in one or two field trips to a factory or a foundry. This version of the history course only lasted for about four or five years, then teachers curtailed the field trips and reduced the concentration on the history of industry (Hopkins, interview). Focus in later years reverted to British history, "especially the battles" (Geddes, interview).

Other academic subjects included geography, where students spent a lot of time drawing maps of different countries; physiography, a mixture of geography and science, with the emphasis on physical geography and climate; chemistry, with an emphasis on conducting experiments; and French, learned through books rather than conversation (Brooks, interview; Brown, interview; Champness, interview).

Students in every course took physical training, though not as frequently as other classes—twice a week or so was normal. Students would change into a gym outfit, with shorts and sometimes a change of tops. At first, the school did not have a gymnasium, so students took their classes outside in good weather. This meant exercises on a cinder court between wings of the school; many students would return home on those days with cinders in their knees. In worse weather, students had the use of a small room in the basement, full of pipes and plumbing (Cull, interview; Hopkins, interview). Later, expansion allowed for two gymnasia—a boys' gym and a girls' gym. The school still had no proper playing field.

Most physical training classes were spent either in floor games (like basketball) or more frequently, in gymnastic exercises—doing exercises, running, tumbling, or using various pieces of equipment. One student recalled,

> Our gym teacher...was an ex-Royal Navy man....He had a cane—a bamboo cane—he called his "persuader."...Now they had ropes tied to the roof of the gym, and you went up them hand over hand. He'd always demonstrate it first, and then you were expected to go up those ropes. Eventually, [you were expected] to get up there at the same time as he could, and if you didn't make it, he'd let you go so far and then you'd get a whack across the rump with the "persuader."
> Now there were always two bells at the end of the class. The first one was a warning bell, which meant that you had to start getting changed out of your gym clothes. And, boy, you had better be out of that change room by the time that second bell rang, because he was in there with that cane. (Kennedy, interview)

In the early years, the school also supported a cadet corps. This was mandatory for all male students, who wore a woollen khaki uniform to practice drill either in the school courtyard or at the nearby armouries during school hours.

For some students, a few additional subjects added variety to their week. Female students in the technical program took a period or two of art each week, though male students did not. Some students, particularly those enrolled in the matriculation program (a part of the technical side of the school), spent some time each week in the library. In academic terms, these extras carried little weight; students (aside from those in the special art course) received no marks for their achievements in gym, library, or art classes (London Technical and Commercial High School Student Record Cards, H.B. Beal Secondary School Archives).

The day's round of classes was broken by the lunch hour. In the earliest years of the school, lunchtime was quite lengthy, lasting one hour and forty-five minutes. Many students went home at lunchtime, often getting a hot meal; those who did not go home ate packed lunches at school. In the 1930s, they could buy chocolate milk at the cost of two tickets for a nickel (Geddes, interview). The physical arrangements changed frequently, with students eating at times in designated classrooms, in special lunchrooms, in the auditorium, or in one of the gyms. Some years saw the boys and girls separated, while other years saw them mixed together.

After completing their meals, students left the school building and mixed with their friends, often walking the streets of downtown London for an hour or so. Students had no choice about leaving the building:

> We weren't allowed to roam in and out of the school at random at lunch hour—the doors were locked. We had time to eat our lunch, and whatever, and then the doors were locked. And you had to stand outside 'till they were open again. (M.F., interview)

During the mid-1930s, the lunch time break was quite long for some senior students. This did not please nearby merchants who felt that the students were a disruption. The storekeepers convinced the city police department to assign two or three constables to walk the area during the lunch break to discourage horseplay and shoplifting (Cull, interview).

The school day ended as it had begun, with students walking, riding, or driving home; in some years, however, not every student left at the same time. The "staggered system," introduced in September of 1933 to handle a crisis in overcrowding, changed the temporal structures of the school day. Rather than having all of the school's students spend the same eight periods a day in the building, Principal Beal and his staff arranged for a twelve-period day. Each student attended for eight of the twelve periods, with the senior students starting early or ending late, while each teacher only taught the same number of periods as usual. Noon hour was still a common time, and first year students had their eight periods scheduled during the traditional teaching hours (Beal, 1934; Cull, interview; London Board of Education, 1933, pp. 245–246; 1934, p. 208).

The teachers did not leave in concert with their charges; most stayed behind to finish paperwork or marking or to prepare for the next day. In addition, many of the teachers seemed willing to take some extra time to help particular students. As one student remembered, "Nothing was too much trouble for them" (Hopkins, interview).

While the prescribed structures, accepted pedagogy, and delivered curriculum described above merit examination in any survey of school experience, revisionist historians and sociologists of education have drawn attention to what they call the "hidden curriculum"—the rules of behaviour enforced at a taken-for-granted level (see, for example, P. Jackson, 1990; Vallance, 1973/1974). In the London Technical and Commercial High School, this aspect of the school experience was pervasive and in fact, openly emphasized—rather than hidden—by school administrators. Discipline at the school was considered to be enforceable in the classroom, between classes, as well as before and after school. Students who misbehaved might receive extra homework, one or more detentions, or (in the case of gym classes) be made to run laps or do extra callisthenics. Others found themselves sent to the principal's office, where they might face the strap or receive detentions along with a lecture on proper behaviour (making the principal primarily a figure of discipline for many students).[22]

> Only major misdemeanours had expulsion from the school, and they had to be major—destroying property or equipment or something, malicious damage, or an incorrigible person, who they couldn't discipline.... Fighting, swearing, vulgarity and smoking were all sort of medium misdemeanours. You might get up to a week's detention or two week's detention if it was really something horrible, or something you repeated. (Cushman, interview)

Attendance too was a regulated behaviour. Students who had good or perfect attendance received a bonus of up to 5 percent on their final average mark, while being late to school was a sure ticket to the detention room (M.F., interview).

Classroom discipline followed certain common rules throughout the school, but ultimately, individual teachers had their own definitions of proper behaviour and their own means of providing censure: "We were always very scared of our teachers.... We wouldn't say 'boo' to them, because they were an authority" (Richardson, interview).

Of one particular teacher, only bad memories seem to remain among all the students interviewed:

> He was a bully, and I don't think he was right, his personality was warped, I'll put it that way. He started every class by slamming a metre stick on the front work table... and that was the way he'd run his class from start to finish, with a loud yelling voice. And he took no, there was no jokes, no kidding, no laughing in his class. He taught very well, because you were scared of him literally, because he would smack fellows on the side of the head and so on like that. I've seen him knock fellows right off their stool. But, he didn't give many detentions, he handled it all himself in his classroom. I didn't, nobody liked him. I guess he taught us—I guess we learned our subject—but it wasn't because he put it across to us in any way of a gentlemen. He was a boor and a bully. (Mitchell, interview)

One aspect of behaviour constantly brought to students' attention was the habit of calling their elders "sir" or "ma'am." The slogan "Get the 'Yes, Sir' habit" appeared on signs in classrooms throughout the school and was repeated constantly by teachers. Many of them told their students that this habit represented a key to the successful reputation of the school and its consequent ability to place students in employment situations.

Discipline extended beyond the classroom walls. As the students moved through the halls in single file, teachers would come out to ensure that order was maintained and that no one was speaking. One of the perennial monitors brought his yardstick with him to enforce his power, though the other teachers refused to follow his example. Principal Beal himself also frequently appeared in the halls to watch his charges. Students caught speaking in the line between classes would be pulled from the line, either silently or with much commotion—depending on the teacher—and sent for punishment.

At times discipline reached even further. As one former student recalled,

> It was a no-smoking school; after school you had to be at least two blocks from the school [before you could smoke]. How they built in these kinds of restrictions…. But that was life as it was then; nobody seemed to think this was a hardship. That's just what the rules were. (Cushman, interview)

Despite the teachers' efforts, not all students conformed to their idea of disciplined behaviour. Some skipped school, others exchanged notes as they passed silently in the halls, while the most outspoken acted disruptively in the classroom. One of the most popular means of misbehaviour was to throw things (peanuts, for instance) at the teacher when his or her back was turned (Brown, interview). Writing rude things on the blackboards or other places in the classroom also proved popular. Nicknames, too, indicated a quiet rebellion. Mr. T. W. Oates became "Timothy Wheat Oats," and Mr. Wheeler, who "had a game leg," was called "side-wheeler" behind his back (Pruss, interview). Students in many courses would try to get away with practical jokes, though the technical students usually had the most access to materials which could serve their pranks. Thus, students in the auto mechanics course would take some carbide (used in early automobile lamps) and drop it into water to generate an awful, pervasive, odour (Cushman, interview).

Other forms of resistance to teachers existed; some used the internal mechanisms of the school:

> We had a Mr. O'Donell, from Dublin. He taught French…. So him and I got into an argument one day, so he put me in the hallway, and I thought "I'm not putting up with this," so I went right upstairs to the office to the principal. And next thing you know, this Mr. O'Donnell is standing looking through the door, so the principal calls him in and he said, "Mr. Pruss will not be in your class any longer." He said, "What's your problem?" I said, "Well you can't understand the man when he talks the King's English, so how do you understand an Irishman from Dublin, teaching you French?" I said, "It sounds like something from some other foreign country." I said, "I just don't get along with him, you leave me in there, why I'll just be in a problem all the time with him." So the rest of them, they caught on, so there's a lot of them got out of the class doing the same thing. Get in an argument with him, and then get out of it. (Pruss, interview)

Students also rebelled at times against the general codes of behaviour, such as that which barred smoking on school grounds:

> We used to smoke in the boiler room. In those days, you know, it was just, girls were just beginning to smoke and that sort of thing. And the man who was in charge of the boiler room, he was very understanding, he let us smoke in there sometimes. (Carter, interview)

The washrooms too often "reeked of smoke," though students would deny their behaviour when challenged by a teacher (Cushman, interview).

The more relaxed atmosphere of physical training class allowed for other forms of rowdy conduct. One student recalls a row of "travelling rings" hanging from the gymnasium ceiling. He and his classmates used to swing from the rings

> like a monkey, going from one end to the other. Our objective was to see if we could get up enough speed at the end rings to be able to get our feet up onto the balcony and grab the rail. Of course this was forbidden, but it was fun. We used to try it. (Cushman, interview)

Even the popular Mrs. Cryderman and her loosely structured art classes did not prove immune from this sort of statement:

> We had a great many life-sized plaster casts of ancient Greek gods, Mercury and Zeus. And sometime when she must have been out of the room ... some of the boys went in and they painted strategic spots with bright colours green. I always remember the fig leaf on—of course there were fig leaves on all of them because it was a school—the leaf on Mercury who is you know, bright, bright green, and I've never seen anyone so angry. She just went into orbit. And I'd never heard her really raise her voice, and she screamed and yelled at us, and stormed up and down the room ... and until whoever did it confessed, she wasn't having anything to do with us, she wouldn't even talk to us. (Carter, interview)

At times, student resistance to certain classroom management techniques left other students as victims:

> We knew we had a squealer in the [science] class. So this day, some of them got in ahead and they went up and got a piece of phosphorus out of the water, and they put it in this kid's desk.... [The teacher] comes whistling and this kid's sitting there and all of a sudden the smoke started coming out of his desk. So he took the kid out in the hall and punished him. But we did it because this kid was squealing on us. (Pruss, interview)

Physical fights between students also broke school rules of conduct, though the immediate reasons were no doubt more personal. Such disputes occurred regularly but usually consisted only of a few blows; more serious fights were often broken up by other students (Cushman, interview).

Finally, not every student was concerned with their performance at school. Other interests, including outside work, often claimed more of their attention.

While students spent their school day in the company of the same group of classmates (usually of the same gender), extracurricular activities allowed students from different years, different classes, and different courses to meet. Some extracurricular activities, such as sports participation, remained segregated by gender, but others provided opportunities for boys and girls to mix either as participants or as spectators. Before the building of the gym and auditorium, the school offered little in the way of extracurricular activities. Unlike later years, there were no sports, dances, or musicals. Despite this, teachers did try to organize a few leisure activities, such as hikes, sleigh rides, or skating parties (Brown, interview; Smith, interview).

In later years, extracurricular sports included basketball for both boys and girls, track and field, sometimes baseball, and boy's hockey (with very little in the way of protective equipment). The school boasted no football team, though. Most sports took place after school; neither players nor spectators were excused from lessons for games. The lack of field facilities meant many of the activities took place at nearby schools with better facilities. Despite these drawbacks, there was still a lot of enthusiasm. In addition, sports participation allowed student athletes a chance to travel to nearby communities for games (Brooks, interview).

Activities concerned with more cultural pursuits also brought students from various courses together. Some thirty to forty students made up the large school orchestra, while the glee club and the literary society provided similar forms of activity. The best-known cultural activities, though, were the annual school shows which commenced with the building of the auditorium. These shows involved hundreds of students, including a large cast, the orchestra, and scores of workers. The facilities available through the technical side of the school—especially carpentry and painting—made the school shows much more impressive than those of other secondary schools in the city. The annual show ran for several nights each spring and usually attracted sell-out crowds.

After the building of the school gym, dances became a regular fixture of the social calendar. The school orchestra would provide the music for waltzes, foxtrots, or jitterbugs. The teachers, acting as chaperones, would lead by example and dance themselves. Strict adolescent social rules governed the behaviour of students at these affairs:

> There'd be a line of boys along one wall and a line of girls along the other wall.... They wouldn't think anything of going over and asking a girl to dance. The girls...didn't ever ask the boys. The girls were not aggressive.... You waited 'till a boy asked you. If you didn't get asked you were considered a "wallflower." (Geddes, interview)

For a while, the school ran annual picnics. Everyone would go to the school building, where the teachers took attendance. Then, they jumped on the open-sided Street railway cars which were waiting, lined up outside the building. The school body reached the park by about ten o'clock in the morning. Following lunch, a program of sports and games took place. In the late 1930s, individual class picnics replaced the more embracing school picnics and often involved more distant destinations, such as Port Stanley on Lake Erie (Cushman, interview).

For senior students, much of their last days at school were occupied with thoughts of the next stage: entrance to the world of work. Even here, school structures were important since the school handled placement duties for many of its students, though not every student benefited. Generally, teachers sent a small group out to interviews after being contacted by an employer needing to fill specific positions. At other times, the school put enquiries around to local employers to see if they would take students. A teacher involved in the relevant area would then decide who to send out for the interviews; obviously, such arrangements added immeasurably to the power available to some teachers, who could exert some control over the subsequent careers and earnings of their charges.

The students chosen would be called to the office and given a couple of days warning. As part of this process, students received instruction on how to behave themselves in interviews. In some cases, the preparation was on an individual basis. But near the end of the year, one of the teachers would address each class of senior students: "the girls were to dress like ladies, and our nails were to be clean, and our hair was to be clean—and the boys were to wear a suit" (M.F. , interview).

Conclusions and Complexities

While the foregoing appears primarily as a mass of thick description, some observations emerge from the account. One central theme in the recounting of the tales of everyday life is the importance of structures in the school. Students spent their day segregated by gender, year, and course. Their experience in academic and commercial classrooms was bound by tight rules of discipline and formal modes of pedagogy. The building of the gym and auditorium wing thus marks an important experiential change, as it allowed for the dissolution of some structures of segregation in terms of sports, the school show, dances, and other extracurricular activities.

The conclusion that schools are highly structured environments is not revolutionary; in fact, for many people, no other phase of life ever comes under such rigid rules. Yet all the structures of schooling had to be continually recreated through the practices of human actors. All the people who spent time in the school, the principal, teachers, students, and support staff, contributed to the ongoing structurisation of school life, as did people who never physically entered the school on a typical day—parents, board officials, employers, and the great mass of people with no direct connection to London Technical and Commercial High School but with a firm sense of what education involved.

In most cases, it is far easier to see teachers and administrators as the agents whose practices reinscribed particular structures, but student behaviour, passive or active, also played a role. Thus, the structured maintenance of gender divisions through course selection, curriculum variation, and coercive control over much student activity also received support from student practices such as wearing gender-distinctive clothing or lining up on opposite walls at the start of school dances (see also Connell, 1982). Similarly, teachers employed at least three distinct pedagogic styles, and a number of different pedagogic practices, yet they all shored up the structured relationship between teacher and pupil; most students accepted the authority of this relationship and even allowed it to govern their behaviour up to two blocks away from the school before or after formal school hours.

Finally, it is clear that all students (and all teachers) were able to act for themselves in some ways, despite the surrounding structures. Student "misbehaviour" can be interpreted in a variety of ways. At one level, acting up served to challenge existing structures, encouraging teachers to abandon some of their role constraints and react as individuals. Such behaviour is part of the continuous bargaining between students and teachers which is crucial to the reproduction or transformation of lived classroom structures. At the same time, student misbehaviour also served to justify and, thus, reproduce the massive disciplinary structures of the school.

Yet dropping phosphorus into a "squealer's" desk or throwing peanuts at a teacher were only the least subtle forms of agency; at a day-to-day level, the senior male students on the technical side had the greatest control over the conditions of their schooling, as each tended to work on an individually chosen project or tackled a different problem as they fixed teachers' cars or tended to the school's practical needs. It is interesting to note that the one example we have of a student challenging fundamental school structures (Glen Pruss' successful campaign to move out of a particular teacher's French class), involved a young man enrolled in the general technical course.

The conclusion that students in shop courses had the greatest control over the conditions of their schooling offers an intriguing sidelight on the normal perception of vocational education. This might explain some of the continuing ambivalence about vocationalism, as opposed to the ongoing acceptance and promotion of more "academic" versions of schooling, among those lobbies which equate social control with education. Certainly, these insights suggest how generative studies at the level of individual schools, particularly those with vocational and academic missions coexisting, can be. Such studies show how structures are not timeless and immutable but are in Williams' (1977) words both "structures of feelings" and "structures of intentions" at once constraining and negotiable, produced and reproduced in an ongoing social process.

Appendix

Appendix: Interview Sources.

Teachers

Name:	Subject:	Starting Year:
Fallona, Margaret	Academics	1930
Morgan, Pearl	Academics	1922

Students

Name:	Course:	Years at LTCHS:
Allison, Marjorie	Special Commercial	1930-1
Brooks, Tom	General Commercial	1931-3
Brown, Gaye*	General Commercial	1920-3
Buchwald, Art	General Technical	1925-8
Carter, Nora	Art	1931-5
Champness, Tom	General Technical	1920-3
Childs, Joyce*	General Commercial	1927-30
Cull, Helen	General Commercial	1922-5
Cushman, Russ	Special Auto Mech.	1934-5
Darnell, Helen	Night School, Cooking	1921-2
"M.F."	General Commercial	1935-8
Fisher, Ben	General Technical	c. 1930
Geddes, Irene	General Commercial	1930-3
Hopkins, Norman	General Technical	1924-8
"M.K."	Special Commercial	1927-8
Kennedy, Harold	General Technical	1935-40
MacDonald, Evelyn	General Commercial	1932-5
Maclaren, Hilda	General Commercial	1928-31
Mitchell, Fred	General Technical	1937-40
Pruss, Glen	General Technical	1933-6
Richardson, Edna	General Commercial	1921-4
Smith, Edith	General Commercial	1924-8
Spence, Gladys	Nursing and Diet.	1930-1
Walsh, George	General Technical	1932-5

* These two students also took secretarial positions at LTCHS after graduating.

NOTES

1. Anstead's research diary was kept over the five-year period of the research work.
2. The use of postmodern arguments has brought this emphasis on the historian's subjective role in creating an interpretation of the past to the fore of historical debate.
3. Of course, the annaliste bow has more than one string. The school also supports those working on "total" history (see, for example, Le Roy Ladurie, 1975).
4. For a discussion of the impact of the stories of Beal and Fallona, see Goodson and Anstead (1993) and Anstead and Goodson (1994).
5. McTavish died, at age fifty, in early 1973 (McTavish, n.d.; *Mr. Integrity*, n.d.).
6. Studies in Curriculum History is a series of twenty-six books published by Falmer Press in the years between 1985 and 1998. Some of this work is summarised in the book *Learning, Curriculum and Life Politics* (Goodson, 2005). More comprehensively, the new book *Leaders in Curriculum Studies* (Short & Waks, 2009) details the emergence of this field in considerable and erudite detail.
7. This description is not yet an accepted interpretation of Canadian history, though some Canadian historians, such as Lenskyj (1983) and Walden (1989), have moved in this direction. Instead, this interpretation draws from the example of American and British historians such as Smith-Rosenberg (1985), Blumin (1985),
8. For instance, according to student record cards from the London Technical and Commercial High School, of the ninety-seven students entering the matriculation program, either directly in first year or by transfer at more senior years for the school years starting in 1927 and 1928, only nine completed the full five years, whereas another eleven completed fourth year.
9. From the 1870s, the Ontario school system included two types of secondary schools: high schools and collegiate institutes. Both taught the normal academic curriculum, with high schools teaching modern languages to males and females and collegiate institutes teaching the classical languages, mainly to young men. By the twentieth century, this distinction no longer existed. High schools and collegiate institutes enrolled students of both genders, whom they taught an academic curriculum on a college preparatory model, though most graduates went into the workforce, not to higher education (Gidney & Millar, 1990).
10. Beal's comments reveal his concern with slotting students into specific occupations—a major goal of the social efficiency movement. On Beal's own commitment to social efficiency, see Goodson and Dowbiggin (1991).
11. Fallona was a student at the school in the 1920s and a teacher in the commercial department in the 1930s.
12. Similar courses were introduced elsewhere in North America. See Kantor (1988, p. 63) for evidence from California.
13. Of course, even in the home of coeducation itself—the United States—a similar pattern held true (see Powers, 1992; Rury, 1984, pp. 36–38; Tyack & Hansot, 1990).
14. On commercial education in the United States, see Weiss (1982); Rury (1984, pp. 29–34); and Powers (1992, chapters 4 and 10).
15. For a parallel account describing how the separate physical location of a department allowed for a separate status, see Labaree (1986, p. 164).
16. The best analyses of social efficiency and its effects on education can be found in Kliebard (1986, pp. 89–122) and in Franklin (1986, pp. 83–118).
17. This happened throughout the province, although other places did not have the excuse of a spectacular fire (see N. Jackson & Gaskell, 1987, p. 194).

18. There is some evidence that local educators had tried to increase male attendance through earlier advertising campaigns. Documents from the period 1914 to 1917 contain a series of references to programs of publicity for commercial education on the part of the principal of the collegiate institute and the commercial advisory committee and with the approval of the board of education. Yet during the same period, the same men (and they were all men) complained that the facilities for commercial classes had become strained to the limit. Why did such an oversubscribed course generate campaigns of recruitment when other courses did not? A logical answer (though one unsupported by surviving direct evidence) is that the campaign was aimed at males, rather than at seeking to increase the absolute numbers of commercial students (see, for example, London Board of Education, 1914, p. 140; 1915, p. 53; 1916, p. 146; 1917, p. 115; 1918, p. 140).
19. On the philosophy behind domestic science, the alternate vocational option for young women, see Pedersen (1981, pp. 178–194); Danylewycz, Fahmy-Eid, and Thivierge (1984, pp. 106–112) and Crowley (1986, pp. 520–521). The Canadian movement was informed and inspired by similar campaigns in Britain and the United States. On these, see Purvis (1985); Yoxall (1913/1965); and Rury (1984, pp. 21–44).
20. This feminization of commercial studies clearly took place at the expense of domestic technical subjects. In 1923, almost twice as many first-year female students chose commercial studies as chose the general domestic curriculum. In later years, the discrepancy grew; the almost 500 young women enrolled in commercial classes in 1930 contrasted sharply with only 147 registered in domestic technical courses. In 1940, the 70 female winners of commercial certificates far outnumbered the 21 female students who took certificates in home economics (London Board of Education Report, 1940, pp. 72–73, London Technical and Commercial High School Student Record Cards, H.B. Beal Secondary School Archives; Ontario Minister of Education, 1930, pp. 352–353). These statistics differ markedly from the rough estimates presented by Danylewycz et al. (1984, p. 103), who claimed that twice as many young women took domestic subjects as commercial studies in technical schools at this time.
21. The table was constructed from the Ontario Minister of Education (1922) report as follows: *Nonmanual* on the table represents the sum of the report categories titled "Commerce," "Law, Medicine, Dentistry, and the Church," and "Teaching." *Skilled manual* is identical to the category title "The Trades," whereas *Manual unskilled* is the same as the category "Labouring Occupations." The categories titled "Agriculture," "Other Occupation," and "No Occupation" from the report were ignored in the construction of the table.
22. Sutherland (1986, pp. 195–201) discusses contemporary elementary school discipline.

REFERENCES

Advisory Vocational Committee, London Board of Education. (1890–1965). *Minutes of the Board of Education for the City of London.* London, ON, Canada: London Board of Education.

Aldrich, R. (1987). Central issues in history of education: An English perspective. *Canadian History of Education Association Bulletin, 4*(3), 17–25.

Andrews, A. (1983, July). *In pursuit of the past: Some problems in the collection, analysis and use of historical documentary evidence.* Paper presented at Whitelands College Workshop "Qualitative Methodology and the Study of Education," London, ON, Canada.

Anstead, C. J. (1991a). *Progress report* [Internal]. London, ON, Canada: University of Western Ontario, Research Unit for Computers and Curriculum Studies.

Anstead, C. J. (1991b). *The Royal Commission on Industrial Training and Technical Education* [Internal report]. London, ON, Canada: University of Western Ontario, Research Unit for Computers and Curriculum Studies.

Anstead C. J. (1994). Field Notes.

Anstead, C. J., & Goodson, I. F. (1994, May). *Telling tales out of school: Oral testimony and the (re)construction of lived classroom experience.* Paper presented at the Qualitative Research Conference, Waterloo, ON, Canada.

Barlow, N., & Robertson, H. J. (1994). *Class warfare.* Toronto, ON, Canada: Key Porter

Baumann, Z. (2001). *The individualised society.* Cambridge, UK: Polity Press.

Beal, H. B. (1934). Staggered classes. *The Tecalogue.* London, ON, Canada: London Technical and Commercial High School.

Berger, C. (1986). *The writing of Canadian history* (2nd ed.). Toronto, ON, Canada: University of Toronto Press.

Bhaskar, R. (1979). *The possibility of naturalism: A philosophical critique of the contemporary human sciences.* Brighton, UK: Harvester Press.

Blumin, S. (1985). The hypothesis of middle-class formation in nineteenth-century America: A critique and some proposals. *American Historical Review, 90*(2), 299–338.

Bourdieu, P., & Passeron, J-C. (1977). *Reproduction in education, society and culture.* London: Sage.

Bowles, S., & Gintis, H. (1976). *Schooling in capitalist America: Educational reform and the contradictions of economic life.* New York: Basic Books.

Canada. (1911–1941). *The census of Canada.* Ottawa, ON, Canada: King's Printer.

Cohen, I. (1990). Structuration theory and social order: Five issues in brief. In J. Clark, C. Modgil, & S. Modgil (Eds.), *Anthony Giddens: Consensus and controversy* (pp. 33–45). London: Falmer Press.

Comaroff, J., & Comaroff, J. (1992). *Ethnography and the historical imagination.* Boulder, CO: Westview Press.

Committee on Aims and Objectives of Education in the Schools of Ontario. (1968). *Living and learning.* Toronto, ON, Canada: Newton.

Connel, R. (1982). *Making the Difference: Schools, families and social difference.* Sydney: George Allen & Unwin.

Cooper, B. (1985). *Renegotiating secondary school mathematics: A study of curriculum change and stability*. London: Falmer Press.

Cremin, L. A. (1961). *The transformation of the school: Progressivism in American education, 1876–1957*. New York: Knopf.

Crowley, T. (1986). Madonnas before Magdalenes: Adelaide hoodless and the making of the Canadian Gibson girl. *Canadian Historical Review, 67*, 520–547.

Curtis, B. (1988). *Building the educational state, Canada West, 1836–1871*. London, ON, Canada: Althouse Press.

Danylewycz, M., Fahmy-Eid, N., & Thivierge, N. (1984). L'enseignement menager et les "Home Economics" au Quebec et en Ontario au debut du 20e siècle: Une analyse comparée. In J. D. Wilson (Ed.), *An imperfect past: Education and society in Canadian history* (pp. 67–119). Vancouver, BC, Canada: University of British Columbia.

Davis, O. L., Jr. (1991). Historical inquiry: Telling real stories. In E. C. Short (Ed.), *Forms of curriculum inquiry* (pp. 77–87). Albany: State University of New York Press.

Davis, R. H. C. (1981). The content of history. *History, 66*(218), 361–374.

Deever, B. (1990, April). *Curriculum change and the process of hegemony in an Appalachian community*. Paper presented at the Annual Meeting of the American Educational Research Association, Boston.

Denzin, N. K. (1989). *Interpretive biography*. London: Sage.

Denzin, N. K., & Lincoln, Y. (1998). *The handbook of qualitative research*. Thousand Oaks, CA: Sage.

Dickinson, J. A. (1935). Commercial education in the London schools. *The Tecalogue*. London, ON, Canada: London Technical and Commercial High School.

Franklin, B. (1986). *Building the American community: The school curriculum and the search for social control*. London: Falmer Press.

Gaffield, C. (1986). Back to school: Towards a new agenda for the history of education. *Acadiensis, 15*(2), 162–190.

Gaskell, J. (1987). Course enrolment in the high school: The perspective of working-class females. In J. Gaskell & A. McLaren (Eds.), *Women and education: A Canadian perspective* (pp. 151–170). Calgary, AB, Canada: Detselig.

Genovese, E. D. (1974). *Roll, Jordan, roll: The world the slaves made*. New York: Random House.

Giddens, A. (1981). *A contemporary critique of historical materialism* (Vol. 1). London: Macmillan.

Giddens, A. (1984). *The constitution of society: Outline of the theory of structuration*. Cambridge: Polity Press.

Giddens, A. (2011). Structuration theory: Past, present and future. In C. G. A. Bryant & D. Jary (Eds.), *Gidden's theory of structuration: A critical appreciation* (pp. 201–221). London: Routledge.

Gidney, R. D., & Millar, W. P. J. (1990). *Inventing secondary education: The rise of the high school in nineteenth-century Ontario*. Montreal, QC, Canada: McGill-Queen's University Press.

Gilbert, V. K. (1972). *Let each become: An account of the implementation of the credit diploma in the secondary schools of Ontario.* Toronto, ON, Canada: Faculty of Education, University of Toronto.

Giroux, H., & Penna, A. (1983). Social education in the classroom: The dynamics of the hidden curriculum. In H. Giroux & D. Purpel (Eds.), *The hidden curriculum and moral education* (pp. 100–121). Berkeley, CA: McCutchan.

Goodson, I. F. (Ed.). (1992). *Studying teachers' lives.* London: Routledge.

Goodson, I. F. (1995). *The making of curriculum: Collected essays.* 2nd ed. London, New York and Philadelphia: Falmer.

Goodson, I. F. (2004). Change processes and historical periods: An international perspective. In C. Sugrue (Ed.) *Curriculum and ideology: Irish experiences international perspectives.* Dublin, Ireland: The Liffey Press.

Goodson, I. F. (2005). *Learning, curriculum and life politics: The selected works of Ivor F. Goodson.* Abingdon, UK: Taylor & Francis.

Goodson, I. F. (2009). Personal history and curriculum study. In E. Short & L. Waks (Eds.), *Leaders in curriculum studies: Intellectual self-portraits* (pp. 91–104). Rotterdam, The Netherlands: Sense.

Goodson, I. F. (2010). Times of educational change: Towards an understanding of patterns of historical and cultural refraction. *Journal of Educational Policy, 25*(6), 767–775.

Goodson, I. F., & Anstead, C. J. (1993). On explaining curriculum change: H. B. Beal, organizational categories and the rhetoric of justification. *The Curriculum Journal, 4*(Autumn), 403–420.

Goodson, I. F., Anstead, C., & Mangan, J. M. (1998). *Subject knowledge: Readings for the study of school subjects.* London: Falmer Press.

Goodson, I. F., & Dowbiggin, I. (1991). Vocational education and school reform: The case of the London (Canada) Technical School, 1900–1930. *History of Education Review, 20,* 39–60.

Goodson, I. F., & Hargreaves, A. (2006). Educational change over time? The sustainability and non-sustainability of three decades of secondary school change and continuity. *Educational Administration Quarterly, 42,* 39–41.

Goodson, I. F., & Lindblad, S. (Eds.). (2010). *Professional knowledge and educational restructuring in Europe.* Rotterdam, The Netherlands: Sense.

Goodson, I. F., & Sikes, P. (2001). *Life history research in educational settings: Learning from lives.* Buckingham, UK: Open University Press.

Harrigan, P. J. (1986). A comparative perspective on recent trends in the history of education in Canada. *History of Education Quarterly, 26*(1), 71–86.

Henretta, J. (1979). Social history as lived and written. *American Historical Review, 84,* 1293–1322.

Higham, J. (1965). *History: Professional scholarship in America.* New York: Prentice Hall.

Hobsbawm, E. J. (1959/1965). *Primitive rebels.* New York: Norton.

Holly, M. L. (1989). *Writing to grow: Keeping a personal professional journal.* Portsmouth, NH: Heinemann.

Houston, S., & Prentice, A. (1988). *Schooling and scholars in nineteenth-century Ontario.* Toronto, ON, Canada: University of Toronto Press.

Jackson, N., & Gaskell, J. (1987). White collar vocationalism: The rise of commercial education in Ontario and British Columbia, 1870–1920. *Curriculum Inquiry, 17*, 177–201.

Jackson, P. (1990). *Life in classrooms.* New York: Teachers College, Columbia University.

Kantor, H. (1988). *Learning to earn: School, work and vocational reform in California, 1880–1930.* Madison: University of Wisconsin Press.

Kantor, H. A., & Tyack, D. (Eds.). (1982). *Work, youth and schooling.* Stanford, CA: Stanford University Press.

Kincheloe, J. (2004). *Critical constructivism.* New York: Peter Lang.

Kincheloe, J. (2005). *Critical pedagogy.* New York: Peter Lang.

Kincheloe, J., & Berry, K. (2004). *Rigour and complexity in educational research: Conceptualising the bricolage.* London: Open University Press.

Kincheloe, J., & Steinberg, S. (1997). *Changing multiculturalism: New times, new curriculum.* London: Open University Press.

Kincheloe, J., & Steinberg, S. (2007). *Cutting class: Socio-economic class and education* (2nd ed.). Lanham, MD: Rowman & Littlefield.

Kliebard, H. M. (1986). *The struggle for the American curriculum, 1893–1958.* London: Routledge.

Kondratieff, N. D. (1984). *The long wave cycle* (G. Daniels, Trans.). New York: Richardson & Snyder.

Kvale, S., & Brinkmann, S. (2009). *Interviews: Learning the craft of qualitative research interviewing* (2nd ed.). Thousand Oaks, CA: Sage.

Labaree, D. (1986). Curriculum, credentials, and the middle class: A case study of a nineteenth-century high school. *Sociology of Education, 59*, 42–57.

Labaree, D. (1988). *The making of an American high school.* New Haven, CT: Yale University Press.

Lazerson, M., & Dunn, T. (1977). Schools and the work crisis: Vocationalism in Canadian education. In H. A. Stevenson & J. D. Wilson (Eds.), *Precepts, policy and process: Perspectives on contemporary Canadian education* (pp. 285–303). London, ON, Canada: Alexander Blake.

Lazerson, M., & Grubb, W. N. (1974). *American education and vocationalism: A documentary history, 1870–1970.* New York: Teachers College Press.

Lenskyj, H. (1983). *The role of physical education in the socialization of girls in Ontario, 1890–1930.* Unpublished doctoral dissertation, University of Toronto, Ontario, Canada.

Le Roy Ladurie, E. (1975). *Montaillou, Village Occitan cle 1294 a 1324.* Paris: Gallimard.

London Board of Education Reports. (1898–1963). London, ON, Canada: Author.

London Technical and Commercial High School. (1921). *Curriculum: Industrial, technical and matriculation courses.* London, ON, Canada: Author.

London Technical and Commercial High School. (1925). *Announcement 1925–26.* London, ON, Canada: Author.

London Technical and Commercial High School. (1929). *The Tecalogue.* London, ON, Canada: Author.

London Technical and Commercial High School. (1933). *Announcement 1933–34.* London, ON,

Canada: Author.

London Technical and Commercial High School. (1934). *The Tecalogue*. London, ON, Canada: Author.

Lowe, G. (1986). Women, work and the office: The feminization of clerical occupations in Canada, 1901–1931. In V. Strong-Boag & A. C. Fellman (Eds.), *Rethinking Canada: The promise of women's history* (pp. 107–122). Toronto, ON, Canada: Copp Clark Pitman.

Macdonald, B. (1991). Critical introduction: From innovation to reform—A framework for analyzing change. In J. Rudduck (Ed.), *Innovation and change* (pp. 1–13). Buckingham, UK: Open University Press.

Malinowski, B. (1967). *A diary in the strict sense of the term*. London: Kegan Paul & Harcourt.

Mann, R. (n.d.). Quo vadis Domini? (Clipping). H.B. Beal Secondary School Archives, London, Ontario, Canada.

McCulloch, G. (2011). *The struggle for the history of education foundations and futures of education*. London: Routledge.

McCulloch, G., & Richardson, W. (2000). *Historical research in educational settings*. Buckingham, UK: Open University Press.

McTavish, M. (n.d.). *A tribute to Ernie McTavish—The man*. Unpublished paper distributed by Ontario Secondary School Teacher's Federation, District Four, London, Ontario, Canada.

Meyer, J. (1980). Levels of the educational system and schooling effects. In C. E. Bidwell & D. M. Windham (Eds.), *Analysis of education productivity* (Vol. 2., *Issues in Macro Analysis*, pp. 15–63). Cambridge, MA: Ballinger.

Miles, M., & Huberman, M. (1994). *Qualitative data analysis: An expanded sourcebook* (2nd ed.). Thousand Oaks, CA: Sage.

Mishler, E. (1986). *Research interviewing: Context and narrative*. Cambridge, MA: Harvard University Press.

Mr. Integrity. (n.d.). Unpublished paper distributed by Ontario Secondary School Teacher's Federation, District Four, London, Ontario, Canada.

Nevins, J. A. (1938). *The gateway to history*. New York: D. Appleton-Century Co.

Ontario Minister of Education. (1920–1942). *Annual report of the Minister of Education*. Toronto, ON, Canada: Legislative Assembly.

Pedersen, D. (1981). The scientific training of mothers: The campaign for domestic science in Ontario schools, 1890–1913. In R. A. Jarrell & A. E. Roos (Eds.), *Critical issues in the history of Canadian science, technology and medicine* (pp. 178–194). Thornhill, ON, Canada: HSTC Publications.

Plummer, K. (2001). *Documents of life 2: An invitation to a crucial humanism*. London: Sage.

Posen, G. (1980). *The office boom: The relationship between the expansion of the female clerical labour force and the response of the public education system, 1900–1940*. Toronto, ON, Canada: Ontario Institute for Studies in Education.

Powers, J. (1992). *The "girl question" in education: Vocational education for young women in the progressive era*. London: Falmer Press.

Purvis, J. (1985). Domestic subjects since 1870. In I. Goodson (Ed.), *Social histories of the secondary curriculum* (pp. 145–176). London: Falmer Press.

Reid, W. (1984). Curricular topics as institutional categories: Implications for theory and research in the history and sociology of school subjects. In I. F. Goodson & S. J. Ball (Eds.), *Defining the curriculum: Histories and ethnographies* (pp. 67–75). London: Falmer Press.

Ringer, F. (1987). Introduction. In D. K. Muller, F. Ringer, & B. Simon (Eds.), *The rise of the modern educational system* (pp. 1–12). Cambridge, MA: Cambridge University Press.

Rinser, S. (1981). Annaliste paradigm? The geohistorical structuralism of Fernand Braudel. *American Historical Review, 86*(1), 63–105.

Rury, J. (1984). Vocationalism for home and work: Women's education in the United States, 1880–1930. *History of Education Quarterly, 24*, 21–44.

Shipman, M. D., Bolam, D., & Jenkins, D. (1974). *Inside a curriculum project.* London: Methuen.

Short, C., & Waks, J. (2009). *Leaders in curriculum studies: Intellectual self-portraits.* Rotterdam, The Netherlands: Sense.

Silver, H. (1992). Knowing and not knowing in the history of education. *History of Education, 21*(Spring), 97–108.

Smith, L. M., Kleine, P. F., Prunty, J. J., & Dwyer, D. C. (1986). *Educational innovators: Then and now.* New York: Falmer Press.

Smith-Rosenberg, C. (1985). *Disorderly conduct.* Oxford, UK: Oxford University Press.

Stamp, R. (1970). *The campaign for technical education in Ontario, 1876–1914.* Unpublished doctoral dissertation, University of Western Ontario, London, Canada.

Stamp, R. (1975). *School days: A century of memories.* Calgary, AB, Canada: McClelland and Stewart West.

Stamp, R. (1982). *The schools of Ontario, 1876–1976.* Toronto, ON, Canada: University of Toronto Press.

Stevens, D., & Cooper, J. (2009). *Journal keeping: How to use reflective writing for learning, teaching, professional insight, and positive change.* Sterling, VA: Stylus.

Sutherland, N. (1986). The triumph of "formalism": Elementary schooling in Vancouver from the 1920s to the 1960s. In R. A. J. McDonald & J. Barman (Eds.), *Vancouver past: Essays in social history* (pp. 175–210). Vancouver, Canada: University of British Columbia Press.

Thompson, E. P. (1968). *The making of the English working class.* Harmondsworth, UK: Penguin.

Tyack, D. (1991). Public school reform: Policy talk and institutional practice. *American Journal of Education, 100*(1), 1–19.

Tyack, D., & Hansot, E. (1990). *Learning together: A history of coeducation in American public schools.* New Haven, CT: Yale University Press.

Vallance, E. (1973/1974). Hiding the hidden curriculum. *Curriculum Theory Network, 4*(Fall), 5–21.

Walden, K. (1989). Speaking modern: Language, culture and hegemony in grocery window displays, 1887–1920. *Canadian Historical Review, 70*(3), 285–310.

Weiss, J. (1978). *Educating for clerical work: A history of commercial education in the United States since 1850.* Unpublished doctoral dissertation, Harvard University, Cambridge, MA.

Weiss, J. (1982). The advent of education for clerical work in the high school: A reconsideration of the historiography of vocationalism. *Teachers College Record, 83*, 613–636.

Williams, R. (1961). *The long revolution.* London: Penguin.

Williams, R. (1977). *Marxism and literature.* Oxford, UK: Oxford University Press.

Wilson, J. D. (1984). From social control to family strategies: Some observations on recent trends in Canadian educational history. *History of Education Review, 13*(1), 1–13.

Wilson, J. D. (1990). The new diversity in Canadian educational history. *Acadiensis, 19*(2), 148–169.

Wineburg, S. (1991). On reading of historical texts: Notes on the breach between school and academy. *American Educational Research Journal, 28*(3), 495–519.

Yoxall, A. (1913/1965). *A history of the teaching of domestic economy.* Bath, UK: Chivers.

Further Reading

Fiala, R. (2006). Education ideology and the school curriculum. In A. Benavot & C. Braslavsky (Eds.), *School knowledge in comparative historical perspective: Changing curricula in primary and secondary education* (pp. 15–34). Hong Kong: Comparative Education Research Centre, University of Hong Kong.

Goodson, I. F. (2006). Socio-historical processes of curriculum change. In A. Benavot & C. Braslavsky (Eds.), *School knowledge in comparative historical perspective: Changing curricula in primary and secondary education* (pp. 211–220). Hong Kong: Comparative Education Research Centre, University of Hong Kong.

Gervirtz, S. (2006). Micro-politics and the examination of curricular practices: The case of school notebooks. In A. Benavot & C. Braslavsky (Eds.), *School knowledge in comparative historical perspective: Changing curricula in primary and secondary education* (pp. 155–170). Hong Kong: Comparative Education Research Centre, University of Hong Kong.

Kamens, D., & Benavot, A. (2006). World models of secondary education, 1960–2000. In A. Benavot & C. Braslavsky (Eds.), *School knowledge in comparative historical perspective: Changing curricula in primary and secondary education* (pp. 135–154). Hong Kong: Comparative Education Research Centre, University of Hong Kong.

Studies in the Postmodern Theory of Education

General Editor
Shirley R. Steinberg

Counterpoints publishes the most compelling and imaginative books being written in education today. Grounded on the theoretical advances in criticalism, feminism, and postmodernism in the last two decades of the twentieth century, Counterpoints engages the meaning of these innovations in various forms of educational expression. Committed to the proposition that theoretical literature should be accessible to a variety of audiences, the series insists that its authors avoid esoteric and jargonistic languages that transform educational scholarship into an elite discourse for the initiated. Scholarly work matters only to the degree it affects consciousness and practice at multiple sites. Counterpoints' editorial policy is based on these principles and the ability of scholars to break new ground, to open new conversations, to go where educators have never gone before.

For additional information about this series or for the submission of manuscripts, please contact:

>Shirley R. Steinberg
>c/o Peter Lang Publishing, Inc.
>29 Broadway, 18th floor
>New York, New York 10006

To order other books in this series, please contact our Customer Service Department:
>(800) 770-LANG (within the U.S.)
>(212) 647-7706 (outside the U.S.)
>(212) 647-7707 FAX

Or browse online by series:
>www.peterlang.com